THE YONITANTRA

The Yonitantra

Critically edited with
an introduction
by

J.A. SCHOTERMAN

MANOHAR
2026

First published 1980
Reprinted 2026

ISBN 978-93-88540-95-7

Published by
Ajay Kumar Jain *for*
Manohar Publishers & Distributors
4753/23 Ansari Road, Daryaganj
New Delhi 110 002

Printed and bound in India

For

BOBBY ORANGE

PREFACE

The *Yonitantra* probably belongs to that kind of Tantric Literature, which gave in the last century and for a long period afterwards Tantrism and its concepts a rather bad reputation. As Sir M. Monier-Williams (1877; repr. 1951, 86) stated: 'Indeed, Tantrism, or Saktism, in Hinduism arrived at its last and worst stage of development', and (id. p. 90): '. . . the Tantras are generally mere manuals of mysticism, magic, and superstition of the worst and most silly kind'.

The basis for a more justified opinion on Tantric literature and the ideas it conveys, was laid by the studies of Sir John Woodroffe and Arthur Avalon in the first part of this century. Gradually, understanding and knowledge grew with Western scholars, until in present times Tantrism has become rather popular with a large audience outside the Indian Subcontinent—a popularity, however, which is mainly based upon those aspects of Tantrism formerly looked on with so much abhorrence.

The *Yonitantra* fits rather nicely into this pattern, dealing with that side of Tantrism which seems to be the most appealing to the average Western adept of Tantric Religion. Although the contents of the *Yonitantra*, now for the first time—critically—edited, may even today give rise to controversy, its importance cannot be ignored. The *Yonitantra* provides information on religious practices which most probably are closely connected with similar practices at Kāmarūpa, but which have remained virtually unknown until today (cf: Bhattacharya, 1971, 16 note 11).

The present edition of the *Yonitantra* is based upon the microfilms of six MSS (vide: Part II), which were acquired by Dr. G. Chemparathy during his stay in Calcutta (1972) on behalf of the 'Deutsche Forschungsgemeinschaft'.

To Dr. T. Goudriaan I wish to express my feelings of sincere gratitude for his useful remarks concerning the subject. The

Institute For Oriental Languages (Utrecht) has kindly permitted me the use of the microfilms and the equipment to read them.

I am very grateful to Mr. A.P. Galestin for his careful correction of my English.

Leiden 1978 J.A. Schoterman

CONTENTS

ABBREVIATIONS

AgniP	*Agnipurāṇa.*
BYT	*Bṛhadyonitantra.*
CVC	*Caturvargacintāmaṇi.*
GŚ	*Gorakṣaśataka.*
HT	*Hevajratantra.*
HYT	*Haṭhayogapradīpikā.*
JAS	*Journal of Asian Studies.*
KP	*Kālikāpurāṇa.*
MNT	*Mahānirvāṇatantra.*
PW	*Petersburger Wörterbuch.*
ṚgS	*Ṛgvedasaṃhitā.*
RASB	The Royal Asiatic Society of Bengal.
RT	*Rādhātantra.*
ṢaṭSS	*Ṣaṭsāhasrasaṃhitā.*
ŚB	*Śatapathabrāhmaṇa.*
ŚS	*Śivasaṃhitā.*
ST	*Samayācāratantra.*
VS	*Vājasaneyiṃhitā.*
ZDMG	*Zeitschrift der Deutschen Morgenländischen Gesellschaft.*
YT	*Yoginītantra.*

THE YONITANTRA

Part I: Introduction

Introduction

I. THE YONITANTRA AND ITS ORIGIN

THE DECISION to study the *Yonitantra*, was actuated by its being mentioned together with the *Mahānirvāṇatantra*, and the *Kālikāpurāṇa*, as one of the three texts held in high esteem at Kāmarūpa (Briggs, 1973, 167). Since the two other texts have been edited and studied to some extent (vide: Bibliography), it seemed useful to study and to edit the *Yonitantra*.

A close relationship of both the *Mahānirvāṇatantra* and the *Kālikāpurāṇa* with *Kāmarūpa* in Assam is plausible. The *Kālikāpurāṇa*—at least in its present recension—'was composed either in Assam or in that part of Bengal, which was very near to it' (Hazra, 1963, 232). The *Mahānirvāṇatantra*, on the other hand, has no direct bearance on Kāmarūpa or Kāmākhyā; the *Tantra* has, however, so much authority—especially among the *Kaulācāryas*—that its predominance in Kāmarūpa is easily understandable.

Five out of the six MSS consulted for the present critical edition of the *Yonitantra*, are written in Bengali script (cf: Part II), a fact which leads to the assumption that at least the copyists were of Northeast Indian origin, particularly Bengal and adjacent regions. In the texts itself, we find references to only two geographical localities: a scarcity which in itself is significant as compared with other *Tantras*. The one reference is to the city of Rājagṛha (V, 20), which is modern Rajgir in Bihar. The other reference, which will turn out to be the most important in determining the origin of the *Yonitantra*, is come across in *Paṭala* IV:

kocākhyāne ca deśe ca yonigartasamīpataḥ //2//
gaṅgāyāḥ paścime bhāge mādhavī nāma viśrutā /
gatvā tatra maheśāni yonidarśanamānasaḥ //3//
ahaṃ cātra niśam devi yonipūjanatatparaḥ /
bhikṣācāraprasaṅgena gacchāmi ca divāniśam //4//
mādhavīyonisadṛśī nāsti yonir mahītale /
tatkucau kaṭhinau durge yonis tasyāḥ supīnatā //5//

We are thus informed that in a country called *Koca*, near *Yonigarta*, on the *paścima* side of the river Ganges, a certain Mādhavī is known to exist; the *Yoni* of this Mādhavī is unequalled on earth; it is the object of constant veneration for Mahādeva, who is the narrator in this fourth *Paṭala* of the *Yonitantra.* The country called Koca is unmistakably modern Cooch Bihar, North of Bangla Desh. The only MS not written in Bengali script, MS A (cf: Part II), reads for *Śloka* 2c *Kaulākhyātapradeśe ca*, instead of *kocākhyāne ca deśe ca.* Although obviously a wrong reading, it is not without importance. Since the MS A is written in modern Kashmiri, its writer might not have been acquainted with Cooch Bihar, which is even today an outlying district, or he may have assumed that his readers did not know the meaning of *kocākhyāne ca deśe ca.* Either way, the writer of MS A opted for the more general designation 'Kaula Country', thus informing his readers that the inhabitants of the region where the *Yoni* of Mādhavī was to be found, were 'Kaula-minded': a valuable piece of information for the prospective pilgrim, who is advised not to enter any country where the *Kaulaśāstra* is prohibited (cf: MNT XI, 148). *Śloka* 3a, *gaṅgāyāḥ paścime bhāge,* is puzzling with regard to Cooch Bihar which is not located at the western part of the river Ganges but north or north-east of the Ganges. The possible translation for this *Pāda,* 'at the last part of the river Ganges', is also not very probable, since this should refer to the delta of the Ganges in modern Bangla Desh. The problem provided by *Śloka* 3a seems to be unsolvable, unless we assume that some local river in Cooch Bihar is called Ganges, or has been identified with the river *par excellence*, the Ganges. The information that the *Yoni* of Mādhavī is located in the vicinity of *Yonigarta* (*Śloka* 2d), is not of much help at first sight: a locality called *Yonigarta*, 'Cave of the *Yoni*', is not accounted for in the texts, as far as we know. A relation with the country called Trigarta - modern Lahore—is hardly acceptable.

In an attempt to find a possible identification of *Yonigarta*, we might turn to Mādhavī Herself. Mādhavī is known to reside at two places: Mathurā (Sircar, 1973, 30 note), and on the mountain *Śrīśaila* (idem, p. 27; 67). Since Mathurā is definitely located in Uttar Pradesh, it can safely be left out of our consideration. The second possible locality, the mountain *Śrīśaila*, provides us with a problem: although a *Śrīśaila* is situated in the Kurnool District, Andhra Pradesh (Dey, 1971, 193), it is a commonly applicable name to any mountain held in high esteem, thus identifying it with the mountain *par excellence*, the Kailāsa.

Recapitulating we have learned so far that on the one hand the Goddess Mādhavī is located in Cooch Bihar near *Yonigarta* (*Yonitantra* IV, 2cd), on the other hand that Mādhavī is believed to reside on the mountain Śrīśaila (Sircar, 1973, 27; 67), which might have been located anywhere in India.

Since Mādhavī, however, is likely to be the female consort of Mādhava—she is actually called *Mādhavapriyā* (Sircar, 1973, 31 note)—we now turn our attention to Mādhava. In the *Yoginītantra*, a text dealing exclusively with the region of Kāmarūpa, we are informed about a *Mādhavāraṇyaka* in Kāmarūpa (Uttarakhaṇḍa I, 30) and about His residence on the mountain *Candrakūṭa* (*Uttarakhaṇḍa* III, 6; IV, 6), east of the Vāyugiri in Kāmarūpa (*Uttarakhaṇḍa* III, 5)[1]. The *Padmapurāṇa* (VI, 129, 12) mentions a *Mādhavatīrtha* on the Śrīśaila. Assuming an interchangeability of the name Śrīśaila with the name Candrakūṭa (cf: Schoterman, 1977, 934), and keeping in mind that Mādhavī is the female consort of Mādhava, it follows that the Goddess Mādhavī resides on the Śrīśaila/Candrakūṭa, a mountain in the region of Kāmarūpa.

The next step is the identification of the locality called Yonigarta in the *Yonitantra*. Possibly, it refers to the shrine of the Goddess Kāmākhyā in Kāmarūpa. A rather plausible assumption

[1](KP LXXIX, 20ab). For *pūrṇavāyugireḥ* (YT *Uttarakhaṇḍa* III, 5a) read: *pūrvaṃ vāyugireḥ*

in view of the fact that the shrine of Kāmākhyā in Kāmarūpa is indeed a cave, called *manobhavaguhā* (YT XI,35), or as the *Kālikāpurāṇa* says: *guhā mānobhavā tatra manobhavaguhā* (LXII, 88). The word *Yonigarta* occurs several times in the *Yonitantra* (I, 15; V, 11 etc.), but there it merely designates a particular part of the vulva. Only in *Paṭala* IV, 2d it might designate Kāmarūpa, or rather the shrine of the Goddess Kāmākhyā.

The fact that the *Yonitantra* claims the *Yoni* of Mādhavī definitely to be located in Cooch Bihar, does not necessarily contradict its identification with the mountain Śrīśaila/Candrakūṭa in Kāmarūpa. In the course of history the boundaries of both areas, Cooch Bihar and Kāmarūpa, have changed constantly (Gait, 1926, 10ff.; Kakati, 1948, 2ff.). The rulers of Cooch Bihar wielded power over Kāmarūpa in the 16th century A.D. King Viśvasiṃha is believed to have rebuilt the temple of Kāmākhyā and to have revived Her worship (Gait, 1926, Ch. IV.) Cooch Bihar and Kāmarūpa are situated so near to each other geographically, that sharing of one another's holy places is not an uncommon feature, especially in case of an enumeration.

The allocation of the shrine of Mādhavī to Cooch Bihar might not be, however, without importance in view of the fact that the *Yonitantra* does not mention anywhere Kāmākhyā nor Kāmarūpa by name: a rather peculiar thing to do for any *Tantra* or *Tantric* text. To this unorthodoxy on the part of the *Yonitantra* we will return later.

The lines we have seen from the *Yonitantra*, describing the *Yoni* of Mādhavī (IV, 2cd-5), we also find, more or less the same, in the *Yoginītantra* (*Paṭala* XIII):

kocākhyāne ca deśe ca yonigartasamīpataḥ /
sādhvī satī brāhmikā hi revatī jaluvismṛtā[2] //2//
mlecchadehodbhavā yā tu yoginī sundarī matā /
tatkucau kaṭhinau dvandvau yonau tasyāś ca pīnatā //3//
bhikṣācāraprasaṅgena gacchāmi ca divāniśam /
tatsannidhau maheśāni tvayā me maraṇaṃ[3] *mahat* //4//

[2]*jalavismṛtā* seems to be corrupt. We suggest the reading *nāma vismṛtā* or *nāma viśrutā*.

[3]For *maraṇaṃ* read: *ramaṇaṃ*, a fairly common permutation in MSS.

Here we deal with the *Yoginī* Revatī instead of Mādhavī, but again located in Cooch Bihar, near *Yonigarta.* The story of the *Yoginī* Revatī is told in the first part of *Paṭala* XIII (1-23). The story runs as follows: When asked by *Devī* about His regular absence, *Īśvara* answers Her that He goes to Cooch Bihar where in the vicinity of *Yonigarta* the *Yoginī* Revatī lives. On *Devī's* request after the antecedents of this *Revatī* (XIII, 5; 6) *Iśvara* tells Her story briefly. Because neither *Iśvara* nor Revatī Herself did experience any satisfaction (*sutṛpti*) from sporting with each other (*rāsakrīḍā*), Revatī went to *Ekāmragaha* to practise austerities. When a Brahmin asked Her for alms one time, She did not respond to his request. For this She was cursed by the Brahmin, who condemned Her to live in foreign parts (XIII, 11: *mlecchatāṃ yāhi durmade*). Because of Her having practiced austerities, *Īśvara* feels Himself attracted towards Her living in exile. The result of this is the birth of their son Venusiṃha.[4] Suddenly, in *Śloka* 18, Mādhavī is mentioned: 'In course of time this Mādhavī, O *Devī*, has become absorbed into My body. Just as the mother of Nandin is My spouse, likewise is this *Yoginī* to be regarded; just as Bhṛṅgarīta is My son, likewise is this Venu born from Me' (XIII, 18; 19). Here, Revatī becomes apparently the same as Mādhavī, Who features in the corresponding passage of the *Yonitantra.* After this exhortation to recognise the *Yoginī* and Her child, *Īśvara* proclaims Venusiṃha and his progeny to be the guardians of the Goddess Kāmākhyā and Her shrine in case there will be another curse upon Kāmākhyā from a Brahmin. This last remark refers to the story of Naraka and the *Muni* Vasiṣṭha (cf: YT, *Paṭala* XII).

The story of Revatī/Mādhavī in the *Yoginītantra* can be regarded as an illustration of a common phenomenon, e.g., the embedding of a foreign/local deity into an established religious system (sc: the worship of Kāmākhyā). In case of a female deity, she is likely to become the wife of the predominant God (h.l: *Īśvara*), or a manifestation of His wife (h.l: *Devī*); their offspring is wont to become 'Guardians of the Faith', as is the

[4]The YT reads always *venu* instead of *veṇu.* The form *venu* might, however, indicate the foreign origin of their son.

case with Venusiṃha. Revatī/Mādhavī being cursed by a Brahmin furnishes a nice parallel with Kāmakhyā Herself: She was forced to leave Her shrine in Kāmarūpa on account of the curse of the *Muni* Vasiṣṭha upon Naraka (cf: YT XII, 14ff.). The assumption that *Revatī/Mādhavī* did not belong originally to the religious system centered around the Goddess Kāmakhyā in Kāmarūpa, can also be deduced from Her being called *asurī* (YT XIII, 8d). Moreover, Her name Revatī is rather vague. Throughout the story She is referred to with non-descript denominations: *yoginī, satī, brāhmikā,* and *sādhvī*. Only once She is called Revatī (XIII, 2b), which is again a non-committal name. Revatī is best known as the wife of Balarāma, and as a *Yoginī* She is mentioned among the 64 *Yoginīs* (Agnip LII, 8; CXVIL, 21; CVC, p. 102).[5] Only at the end of the story it seems Her real name, Mādhavī is mentioned, when *Īśvara* urges *Devī* to accept Mādhavī and Her son Venusiṃha (vide supra). It is very plausible that the story told in connection with the *Yoginī* Revatī/Mādhavī in the *Yoginītantra*, refers to the Mādhavī of the *Yonitantra*. Again the name *Yonigarta* is significant, assuming that it denotes Kāmarūpa. The *Yoginītantra*, which is a glorification of the Goddess Kāmākhyā and Her shrine in Kāmarūpa, mentions the names Kāmākhyā and Kāmarūpa almost everywhere; only in this single instance (XIII, 2b) *Yonigarta* might be used instead of Kāmarūpa. This leads to the hypothesis, that the lines which the *Yoginītantra* and the *Yonitantra* have in common, might have been borrowed from the latter for the purpose of embedding the Goddess Mādhavī into the religious system around Kāmākhyā. It is significant, though, that in doing so, the *Yoginītantra* changes Her name in the first instance to the vague denomination Revatī (XIII, 2d). Only once the *Yoginītantra* calls Her by real name, Mādhavī, but in an important context: when this *Yoginī* has to be accepted as the spouse of *Īśvara*.

Besides the reference to Cooch Bihar in *Śloka* 2a, there might be another indication in this passage to the same region. In *Śloka* 3a the *Yoginī* Revatī is called *mlecchadehodbhavō*,

[5]Paṇḍit Kanhaiyālālamiśra, who translated the YT into Hindi, takes *Yoginī* as her name.

'Sprung from the body of a foreigner/barbarian'. This designation fits, of course, nicely in the story about Her being exiled. In connection, however, with Cooch Bihar, it might have a special connotation. It is very tentative to see in the designation *mlecchadehodbhavā* a reference to the Mech-tribe, which is identical or at least closely related with the Koches (cf : Gait, 1926, 36; 46; 247): 'The progenitor of the Koch kings was a Mech or a Koch - it is not certain which— ...' (Gait, 1926, 48).

The unique occurrence of the name *Yonigarta* as a designation for Kāmarūpa, both in the *Yonitantra* and the *Yoginītantra* has to be regarded in close context. The *Yonitantra*, which does not mention Kāmākhyā nor Kāmarūpa anywhere by name, is a text dedicated exclusively to the worship of Mādhavī, a local Goddess in Cooch Bihar. The fact that neither Kāmākhyā nor Kāmarūpa are mentioned by name, may point to a certain rivalry between the cult of Mādhavī and Kāmākhyā. The *Yoginītantra*, which mentions Kāmākhyā and Kāmarūpa throughout the text, uses only in this passage corresponding with the *Yonitantra*, the term *Yonigarta* as a designation for Kāmarūpa. This leads evidently to the assumption that the passage in the *Yoginītantra* might have been borrowed from the *Yonitantra* for the sole purpose of making Mādhavī one of the manifestations of the Goddess Kāmākhyā.

Thus, summarizing this section on the origin of the *Yonitantra*, we conclude that the Yonitantra finds its origin in the region of Cooch Bihar near *Yonigarta*/Kāmarūpa, centring around the cult of Mādhavī.

II. MĀDHAVĪ AND VIṢṆU

In an attempt to account for the conspicuous absence of the names of Kāmākhyā and Kāmarūpa in the *Yonitantra*, we next turn our attention to Mādhavī Herself. Although Mādhavī is one of the thousand names of Rādhā (RT, *Paṭala* XXXIII), the name Mādhavī is primarily a designation for the Earth (cf: Bhattacharya, 1971, 24; 1974, 56). In this aspect Mādhavī is connected with Viṣṇu (Bhattacharya, 1974, 24), to whom—

especially as *Vasudeva*—is then given the epithet *Madhu* or *Mādhava* (Gonda, 1969, 16). In this context Mādhavī, and Kāmākhyā who is fundamentally also regarded as the Earth, stand on the same line; a fact which makes the identification of Mādhavī with Kāmākhyā in the *Yoginītantra* very easy. The difference between the two Goddesses, Mādhavī and Kāmākhyā, may perhaps be found in the fact, that Mādhavī of a *Yonitantra* has a *Vaiṣṇava* background while Kāmākhyā has to be placed in a *Śaiva* context.

Even in the *Yoginītantra* we find a reference to a possible *Vaiṣṇava* background of Revatī/Mādhavī : when *Īśvara* tells *Devī* there was no great satisfaction for Him while sporting with Revatī, the word used in the text is *rāsakrīḍā* (YT XIII, 8a), which has a strong *Vaiṣṇava* implication (cf : *Bhāgavatapurāṇa* X, 33, 1ff;).

Although *Yonitantra* has certainly an outward appearance which looks definitely *Śaiva*, being an interlocution between *Mahādeva* and *Devī*, yet there are strong indications for its having a *Vaiṣṇava* inclination. Twice (I, 6a; IV, 10a) the name of Hari/Viṣṇu is placed before the name of Hara/Brahmā, instead of the more usual order as in *Paṭala* VI, 12a; in *Paṭala* I, 6a the *Pāda* has nine syllables—*hariharādyāś ca ye devāḥ*—, which MS A 'corrects' into *harer ādyāś ca ye devaḥ*, thus dropping the name of *Hara*. In *Paṭal* III, 9c we have opted for the reading *mahāśaṅkhena* (MS A: *mahāśakhena*) instead of the non-committal reading *mahāśaktyena* (MSS C, E, F); the *śāṅkha* being a well-known attribute of Viṣṇu. References to *Kṛṣṇa/Rādhā* and *Rāma/Sītā* are found at two instances (IV, 6cd-9; V,19). Instead of *mahādeva* (IV, 8c), two MSS (D, F) read *mahāviṣṇu*. It s possible for the *Sādhaka* to become *Viṣṇu* Himself (IV, 4ab). Instead of *triṣu lokeṣu* (VIII, 1b), two MSS (B, E) read *viṣṇuloke*. The above-mentioned examples, although perhaps circumstantial, point to a *Vaiṣṇava* background of the *Yonitantra*. The next two examples are more decisive, not in the least because the MSS are unanimous. In *Paṭala* VI, 34 cd; 35 the *Vaiṣṇava Pūjā* is said to be a component of the *Yonipūjā*. In *Paṭala* VIII, 32 the *Sādhaka* who performs the *Yonipūjā*, is advised to perform the *Vaiṣṇava Pūjā* in case he should be watched by an outsider, thus concealing the real object of his *Pūjā*; this advise, however, presupposes on the part of the *Sādhaka* a knowledge of this *Vaiṣṇava Pūjā*.

III. VIṢṆU AND THE YONI

We have seen a relation between Viṣṇu and Mādhavī/the Earth, and a possible Vaiṣṇava inclination of the *Yonitantra.* Next we will make some remarks with regard to the relation between Viṣṇu and the *Yoni*, a relation which is accounted for as early as the Vedic period (ṚgS X,184,1: *víṣṇur yónim kalpayatu*).

In *Paṭala* III of the *Yonitantra* we find the lines:

yoni yonīti yo vakti japakāle ca sādhakaḥ /17//
tasya yoniḥ prasannā syād bhuktimuktipradāyinī/

'The *Sādhaka* who utters the words '*Yoni Yoni*' at the time of prayers, for him the *Yoni* shall be favourable, granting him enjoyment and liberation'. The *Yonitantra* does not add anything further. Lines of the same portance we also find in the *Bṛhadyonitantra* (BYT; Folio 3B):

yoni yonīti yo vakti pūjākāle ca varānane/
prasannā tasya yoniḥ syāt saṃtuṣṭā sarvadevatā/

The *Bṛhadyonitantra,* however, explains the origin of the utterance '*Yoni Yoni*'. It was Viṣṇu, or rather Kṛṣṇa, who was the first to utter the words '*Yoni Yoni*'. The whole idea centres around the epithet *bhagavat* of Vīṣṇu/Kṛṣṇa. The pun is, of course, found in the meaning of *bhaga* in the compound *bhagavat,* 'possessing *bhaga*'. Although *bhaga* means in this connection 'Fortune, Prosperity', in the *Bṛhadyonitantra* it is a synonym for *Yoni* as is probably the case in words as *bhaginī* (Gonda, 1953, 23-25)· In this way Kṛṣṇa has the epithet 'The One with a *Yoni*'. *Devī* wonders why Kṛṣṇa obviously being a male, is thus allotted a *Yoni* (BYT F. 4A : *kṛṣṇaḥ svayaṃ mahādeva bhagavān puruṣa ucyate*). *Īśvara* then explains this apparent contradiction: 'In former times the residents of the Heavens desired to descend up to the earth. For this reason they started to praise

Jaganmayī, who granted the request, however, only to Mahāmāyā. She subsequently descended to the earth in a male form after having placed Her *Yoni* in the tail-feathers of a peacock. Next, He/She entered the womb of Devakī, and was born as Kṛṣṇa. One day when dallying with Rādhā and the *Gopīs* in beautiful Vṛndāvana, Kṛṣṇa recognised in the tail-feathers of a peacock His/Her own *Yoni*, and He placed the tail-feathers on His head (*svayonīti viniścitya dhṛtavān śikhare tadā*)'. Thus *Īśvara* explains the reason why Kṛṣṇa is called *bhagavat*, and why He wears the tail-feather of a peacock on His head (cf: Gīta Govinda, 1976, plates III-V). The wearing of peacocks' feathers on the head was already noticed by the Chinese pilgrim Hsüan Tsang during his travels in India: Hsüan Tsang mentions a kind of ascetics wearing the tail-feathers of a peacock on their heads (cf: Beal, 1957-8, II, 134). The connection between the tail-feathers of a peacock and the *Yoni* is probably based upon the design on the tail feathers: the 'eyes' on the feathers resemble a *Yoni*. In the story of *Indra Sahasrākṣa* we find the same similarity between the 'eye' and the *Yoni*: cursed by the *Muni* Gautama, Indra was covered with a thousand *Yonis*, afterwards changed to eyes.

Another connection between Viṣṇu and the *Yoni* is told in the *Tripurārahasya*. In *Paṭala* XXXIV, 54ff. we find the story of *Śivas Liṅga* falling to the earth. When Brahmā sees the *Liṅga* heading for the earth, he urges Viṣṇu with the words:

etal liṅgaṃ yadi patec chūlinaḥ pṛthivītale/
śatadhā pṛthivī śīrṇā bhaviṣyati na saṃśayaḥ / /55//
nāsty anyo dhārako loke vidyate tvām ṛte hare /
yonyākṛtyā dhārayaitat kṣobhaśāntyai na cānyathā //56//

'In case this *Liṅga* of *Śūlin* (=*Śiva*) should hit the earth, she (= the earth) will undoubtedly be scattered into a hundred pieces. You, O Hari, are the only one to receive it: in the form of a *Yoni* receive this *Liṅga* to undo the force of the impact—there is no other way-out!'. Evidently, Viṣṇu is requested by Brahmā to rescue the earth by assuming the form of a *Yoni*. The word *dhāraka* (*Śloka* 56a) is significant in this context: although *dhāraka* might denote any receptacle or vessel, here it is probably a designation for the *Yoni*. In the *Vājasaneyīsaṃhitā*

(XXIII, 22) the word *dhárakā* denotes the vulva, especially when the *Liṅga* has been inserted into it (cf: *Mahīdhara*). Although the *Tripurārahasya* uses the masculine form of the word, the meaning of the feminine *dhárakā* is certainly implicated. The word *dhárakā* seems to be restricted to the Vedic period, where is occurs only twice (VS XXIII, 22=ŚB XIII, 2, 9, 6; and ŚB XI, 6, 2, 10).

Returning for a moment to explanation of the epithet *bhagavat* of Kṛṣṇa (vide supra), it is perhaps useful to remark on another explanation of the same word. In the *Rādhātantra* this epithet of Kṛṣṇa is also a point of discussion. Here *bhaga* is regarded as a synonym for *bhāga* (=part, portion). Because Kṛṣṇa is an *amśa* (=part, portion) of Vasudeva, He is given the epithet *bhagavat* (RT XVIII, 27ab), and is the *Rādhātantra* itself called *Bhāgavata Tantra* (RT XVIII, 30ab) thus putting it on the same line as the *Vaiṣṇava* text *par excellence*, the *Bhāgavatapurāṇa*.

The relation of Viṣṇu with the *Yoni* is also expressed in ritual proceedings. In this context Viṣṇu is closely related to the flower of the *Aparājitā*. The *Aparājitā* is also called *Viṣṇukrāntā* (BYT F.4B: *viṣṇukrāntāsi devi latārūpā bhagavatī svayam*), or simply *Vaiṣṇavī* (ṢaṭSS F. 365B). Moreover, the *Vaiṣṇavī* is the manifestation of the fourth of the *Aṣṭamātṛkās*: *Vaiṣṇavī* (ṢaṭSS F. 365B).

The *Aparājitā* is a creeper with a deep blue flower (Lowis, 1878, Plate X), or *kṛṣṇapuṣpā* (ṢaṭSS F. 365B): the relation with Kṛṣṇa is clear. The Latin name, *Clitoria Ternatea*, is obviously based upon its appearance, as is the English name, Mussel-Shell Creeper: 'the English name, I imagine, has been suggested by its shape and deep colour, as it recalled the rich look of a polished mussel shell' (Lowis, 1878, Plate X)—a comparison belonging to the Victorian era. The deep blue colour of its flower can also be connected with Kāmākhyā Herself: Her mountain in Kāmarūpa is called the *girir nīlābhidhojjvalaḥ* (YT XI, 34b). In the *Bṛhadyonitantra* (F. 4B) we find the story about the origin of the Aparājitā creeper: when Mahāmāyā deposited Her Yoni in the tail-feathers of a peacock (vide supra), from them the *Aparājitā* originated on earth. In connection with the story about Kṛṣṇa being called *bhagavat* in the *Bṛhadyonitantra*, the relation between Kṛṣṇa and the *Aparājitā* becomes clear.

Besides the relation between Kṛṣṇa and the *Aparājitā* as we have seen above, the *Aparājitā* itself can have a specific function in ritual, based on its having the shape of a *Yoni*. The *Aparājitā* is called *bhagavatī* (BYT F. 4B), or its flower is designated as 'having the natural form of a *Yoni* (BYT F.4B: *yonisvarūpa*). Based on this characteristic shape of its flower, the *Aparājitā* is a substitute for the *Śakti* in ritual. Although the *Aparājitā* is not mentioned by name in the *Yonitantra*, we are informed about its function in the *Bṛhadyonitantra*:

yonyābhāve maheśāni yonirūpāparājitām/
pūjayet sādhakaśreṣṭho yonipūjāphalaṃ labhet / (Folio 3B)

or:

maithunaṃ jāyate tena śaktyābhāve'pi sundari / (Folio 4B)

The latter example from the *Bṛhadyonitantra* points to the connection of the *Aparājitā*-flower (sc: *tena*) with that of the *Karavīra*: in combination they represent *Yoni* and *Liṅga*, or *Maithuna* (cf : Avalon, 1972, 109 note 4). In the *Samayācāra-tantra* (ST; F.11A) the *Aparājitā* and the *Karavīra* are mentioned together with other plants as substitutes for the *Yoni* and the *Liṅga*.

IV. THE YONITANTRA AND KĀMARŪPA

In the preceding sections we have shown a close connection between the worship of Mādhavī in Cooch Bihar and the worship of Kāmākhyā in Kāmarūpa. This connection is not opposed by the *Vaiṣṇava* background of the first: both Goddesses are fundamentally to be regarded as manifestations of the Earth, the *Yoni par excellence*: the one being *Vaiṣṇava*, the other *Śaiva*. Moreover, the male counterpart of Mādhavī, Mādhava/Viṣṇu is also closely connected with the *Yoni*, as we have seen. The male counterpart of Kāmākhyā is, of course, *Kāma*. Again, between *Kāma* and Viṣṇu the relation is accounted for (cf: Gonda, 1969, 17). In the *Viṣṇusahasranāmāvali*, a part of the *Gayāmāhātmya*,

Viṣṇu is in fact called Kāma (No. 340), or Kāmadeva (No. 651). The same proves true with regard to Mādhava, who is called Kāma and Kāmālaya (KP XXXVI, 19b). Besides this, one should keep in mind that the history of Kāmākhyā and Kāmarūpa has a strong connection with *Viṣṇuism* from its very beginning: it was the *Asura* Naraka, son of Viṣṇu and Pṛthivī, who received from his father Kāmarūpa for his kingdom and was told by Viṣṇu to worship the *Yoni* of Kāmākhyā (YT XII, 5).

V. THE KULĀCĀRA

We have seen that the *Yonitantra*, a text sprung from *Vaiṣṇava* circles, has been drawn into the *Śaiva* environment of Kāmākhyā by the *Yoginītantra*, a *Śaiva* text. The *Yonitantra* itself seems to seek a more general acknowledgement, promoting itself outside its *Vaiṣṇava* limitations but not directly associating itself with its *Śaiva* counterpart—the *Yonitantra* does not mention anywhere Kāmākhyā nor Kāmarūpa by name. For promoting itself beyond its *Vaiṣṇava* limitations, we find in *Paṭala* IV, 12cd-27ab of the *Yonitantra* a so-called *Kulamāhātmya*, 'A Glorification of the *Kulācāra*', which seems to be very much inspired by the second *Ullāsa* of the *Kulārṇavatantra.*

The exact meaning of the word *kula* and its derivations used in this context remains still doubtful, and is subject for many interpretations. The idea, however, conveyed by such terms as *Kulācāra*, *Kulamārga*, etc., is made clear by the following lines: 'Just as (all) the rivers empty themselves, directly or indirectly, into the ocean, in the same way all the Doctrines meets in the *Kula*-system. Just as the footprint of an elephant can encompass the footprint of every living being (due to its size, of course), likewise all the sects are encompassed within the *Kula*-system' (*Kulārṇavatantra* II, 12; 13). The *Kula*-system surpasses the limitations of the individual systems, uniting them in one all-embracing system, the *Kulācāra*. Or, as Avalon (1972, LXXXII) puts it: 'The Kaula-dharma is in no wise sectarian, but, on the contrary, is the heart of all sects'. We are aware of the fact, that there are many other interpretations of the conception

Kulācāra etc., but for the moment we will deal with the above-mentioned interpretation based on the *Kulārṇavatantra*.

In the *Yonitantra* (IV, 20) we find the well-known lines, which seem to belong to a common (*Kaula*) 'fond':

> *antaḥ śāktāḥ bahiḥ śaivāḥ sabhāyām vaiṣṇavāḥ matāḥ/*
> *nānārūpadharāḥ kaulāḥ vicaranti mahītale//*

'Privately a *Śākta*, outwardly a *Śaiva*, among people a *Vaiṣṇava*; bearing various outward appearances, the followers of the *Kula*-system spread over the earth'. The same *Śloka* we find, among others, in the *Śyāmārahasya* (Wilson, 1862, I, p. 254, note 1), and is quoted by Avalon (1972, LXXXII) without mentioning the text, unfortunately. Although the meaning of the *Śloka* is clear, its second *Pāda* (*sabhāyāṃ vaiṣṇavāḥ matāḥ*) seems to be an addition only for the purpose of including the *Vaiṣṇavas*. The antithesis *antaḥ/bahiḥ* is almost inevitable, but its combination with *sabhāyāṃ* has an artificial ring to it. Although Avalon accepts the *Śloka* without comment, he deems it necessary to comment on the expression *sabhāyāṃ*, translating it with 'gatherings': 'The Vaiṣṇavas are wont to gather for worship, singing the praise of Hari, etc.' (Avalon, 1972, LXXXII, note 1). In the *Śamayācāratantra* (F. 14B), a text which has only one side-way reference to the *Kula*-system (F. 8AB), we find a similar Śloka, but not mentioning the *Vaiṣṇavas*, nor the *Kaulas*:

> *antaḥ śāktāś ca subhage bahiḥ śaivāś ca sudṛḍāḥ /*
> *evaṃ ye sādhakāḥ loke phalaṃ yānti hy asaṃśayam /*

Comparing the Ślokas of the *Samayācāratantra* and the *Yonitantra*, one might assume that the *Vaiṣṇavas* are only mentioned when the *Kaulācāra* is discussed: an assumption which agrees with the idea incorporated in the term *Kulācāra*, being a system superior to sectarian distinctions.

Discussing Tantrism, Śaktism, etc., one is seriously handicapped by the fact that these terms lack a clear definition. Consequently, the exact relationship and difference with 'everyday' Viṣṇuism or Śivaism remains still rather vague. Although quite a number of texts designate themselves as *Tantra*, it is evident that there exists a considerable discrepancy within these '*Tantras*', regarding topics dealt with etc. In this context it is hazardous to say anything definite about a *Tantra* with a *Vaiṣṇava* background like the *Yonitantra*, and its relation to the *Kulācāra*. Although this is not the place to deal with the subject in extenso, some remarks of a general significance might be made, however.

Tantric Literature has from the beginning been connected by Western scholars with Śivaism and Śaktism. The fact that there exists also a *Vaiṣṇava* Tantric Literature, is only mentioned in passing. On *Śaiva* Tantric Literature some research has been done, but since the great majority of the texts lacks a critical edition—if edited at all—the results of this research must be put in their proper context. *Vaiṣṇava* Tantric Literature is at best mentioned, but its contents remain virtually unknown. *Vaiṣṇava* Tantric Literature seems, however, to be of a relatively later date. The style of the *Vaiṣṇava* Tantras appears to be borrowed from their *Śaiva* counterparts. Moreover, they are of a definite *Śaiva* outlook, being often an interlocution between *Īśvara* and *Devī* (e.g. *Gautamīyatantra*, *Sanatkumāratantra* a.o.). Viṣṇuism did develop its own literature rather early (*Bhāgavata-purāṇa*, 10th century A.D.)' culminating in the writings of *Caitanya* (A.D. 1486-1533). The whole bulk of this *Vaiṣṇava* literature, however, falls outside the scope of what might be called Tantric Literature, although connections—the *Vaiṣṇava Sahajīyā*—are certainly accounted for (cf: Dimock, 1966). The establishment of *Vaiṣṇava* Tantric literature can be attributed to the late Medieval Period (13th century, and onwards), especially the post-Caitanya centuries. Favoured by the conditions of time (Dimock, 1966, 26), Viṣṇuism developed its own Tantric literature based primarily upon the *Śaiva* examples available at the time. The development of *Vaiṣṇava* Tantric literature may have served a double purpose: to gain a general acknowledgement against the *Śaiva* Tantric literature—as in the case of the *Yonitantra*—and at the same time to secure its survival.

Although the above-sketched outline is only a very superficial one and by no means decisive, it might assert itself in due course when more Tantric texts—especially *Vaiṣṇava*—have been critically edited and studied in mutual relationship.

To adopt the outward appearance of a Tantra, the *Yonitantra* opens with a well-known line (I, lab). Immediately after that, the *Yonitantra* classifies itself among the traditional number of sixty-four Tantras. Although the names of these sixty-four Tantras are subject to considerable differences in the various lists, the *Yonitantra*, however, does not figure in any of these lists. On one occasion the *Yonitantra* is mentioned together with several other Tantric texts: the *Nīlatantra* (F. 17B) mentions the *Yonitantra* on the same lines as the *Bhairavatantra* and the *Kulārṇavatantra* in an enumeration of Tantric texts. In the division of the Tantras over the three regions *Viṣṇukrāntā*, *Rathakrāntā*, and *Aśvakrāntā*, the *Yonitantra* is allotted to the first region, the *Bṛhadyonitantra* to the second (cf: Avalon, 1952, 87ff.). In *Paṭala* IV, 12cd-14cd the *Yonitantra* inserts some well-known lines (cf: *Kulārṇavatantra* II, 7ff.) to account for the superiority of the *Kula*-system. Furthermore, the enumeration of the nine classes of *Śaktis* (II, 3ab ff.) seems to have been included for the sake of a Tantrik outlook (vide VI.1).

VI. THE YONIPŪJĀ

1. THE ŚAKTI

The *Yonitantra* (II, 3; 4ab) enumerates nine kinds of women whose *Yōni* is suitable for performing the *Yonipūjā*: 1) an actress (*naṭī*), 2) a woman of the *Kapālika*-order (*kāpālikā*), 3) a prostitute (*veśyā*), 4) a washerwoman (*rajakī*), 5) the daughter of a barber (*nāpiṭāṅganā*), 6) a Brahmin woman (*brāhmaṇī*), 7) the daughter of a *Śudra* (*śudrakanyā*), 8) the daughter of a cowherd (*gopālakanyakā*), and 9) the daughter of a garlandmaker (*mālākarasya kanyā*). These nine women are referred to in the *Yonitantra* as the '*Nava Kanyāh*, (II, 4d), thus telling that they should be unmarried, but not virgins (*kumārī*). This conditoin of not being a virgin on part of the *Śakti*, is stressed upon in *Paṭala* III, 25cd; 26: 'One should worship the *Yoni* of a woman, never that of a virgin; in the latter case there is the loss of supernatural powers (*siddhi*) every time'.

The necessity for the *Sādhaka* to choose his *Śakti* from among the nine specified women, however, is dropped immediately after the enumeration: 'Or she may belong to any caste, as long as she is experienced and wanton' (II, 4cd). Generally speaking, *maithuna* is ordained with every woman (VII, 8ab). There is but one restriction: the *Sādhaka* should never perform the *Yonipūjā* with a mother (II, 5a; cf:YT VI, 44a). The rule as to the *Śakti* being an unmarried woman (*kanyā*) does not hold: she may either be the *Sādhaka's* own wife or somebody else's (I, 14ab; VI, 2ab), but the latter seems to be the most preferable (VII, 17ab). In this context one should keep in mind that although *kanyā* usually denotes an unmarried girl, it may also refer to a married woman: in the Balinese *Smarastava 'Pañca-kanyam,'* the five *kanyās* are Ahalyā, Draupadī, Sītā, Tārā and Mandodarī, which were all married women (Goudriaan and Hooykaas, 1971, No. 037). In Bengal this same *Stava* is recited during the early morning rites. Especially mentioned as *Śaktis* are the female pupil of the *Sādhaka* (IV, 29d; VI, 2d; VII, 30a), ones sister (IV, 29c), or a newly wed woman (IV, 29b; VII, 30b). Perhaps after not being a virgin, the next most important quality of the *Śakti* is that she has not delivered a child. This may be deduced from the three kinds of *Śakti* mentioned above, and from II, 5a, where *maithuna* with a *mātṛyoni* is forbidden. This condition of being childless on the part of the *Śakti* is also known from other texts dealing with the same subject. The *Bṛhadyonitāntra* (F. 2B) prohibits explicitly the use of a woman who has delivered, as a *Śakti*; the *Samyācāratantra* (F. 10A) advises a childless woman: *aprasūtā viśeṣeṇa pañcamārthā bhavet priye* (*pañcama=maithuna*, the fifth *MA-kāra*). Although the *Sādhaka* is allowed to worship the *mātṛyoni*, he should not perform *māithuna* with it (*Yonitantra* V, 13abff.).

Thus the enumeration of the '*Nava Kanyāḥ*' and its implications for the *Śakti*, does not seem to be of any practical importance in the *Yonitantra* when it states that any woman might do for a *Śakti* except a mother. When dealing with *Śaktis*, a Tantra usually provides a list similar to the one in the *Yonitantra*. The inclusion of this list in the *Yonitantra*, where it has no value at all, seems only to indicate the purpose of giving the text a Tantric appearance (cf: V). Moreover, exactly the same list we find in the well-known *Rudrayāmalatantra*[6] (Wilson, 1862, I, 258 note 1). Furthermore, although a Brahmin woman is included, there is some restriction with regard to this kind of *Śakti* (V, 15): the *Sādhaka* is allowed to take her *Yonitattva* (vide: VI.5), but he should worship with it the *Yoni* of another woman. Also in the *Yoginītantra* (VI, 47) the *Brāhmaṇī* is excluded, but here together with a *Kṣatriyā* and a *Vaiśyā*.

The next thing we learn from the *Yonitantra* with regard to the *Śakti* concerns her age: the *Śakti* should be between twelve and sixty years old (II, 5cd). The utmost age of sixty for the *Śakti* seems hardly in agreement with the very nature of the ritual we are dealing with (cf: VI.5). The *Samayācāratantra* (F. 10A) shows much more sense of reality, prescribing the *Śakti* to be between thirteen and twenty-five years of age. The age of twelve, however, is significant. After her twelfth year a girl is generally believed to become a woman when she starts having her monthly periods. As we will see in the section on the ritual of the *Yonipūjā* (VI.5), ritual coition of the *Sādhaka* with his *Śakti* during her *menses* forms an integral part of the *Yonipūjā*. The Bauls of Bengal, who know a similar ritual, express it very delicately in one of their songs as quoted by Capwell (1974, 262):

> The flower blooms after twelve years,
> month after month that flower falls.
> To whom shall I speak about that flower?
> Except for the enlightened, it is forbidden to say.

Summarizing, it is evident that there are hardly any restrictions in the *Yonitantra* with respect to the *Śakti*. As long as she is no virgin and no mother, the *Sādhaka* is free to choose as his *Śakti* any woman between the age of twelve and sixty. That not every text dealing with the *Yonipūjā* is that much lenient, may be seen, for instance, from the *Bṛhadyonitantra* (FF. 2B; 3A): the *Śakti* should not suffer from severe diseases,

[6]There also exists a modern *Rudrayāmalatantra* by Pandit Rāmacaraṇanandarāmaśarma (Bombay, 1955), which is a different text.

nor should her *Yoni* be of a bad smell; the *Sādhaka* is not allowed to select a female slave as his *Śakti*. The first two rules are, obviously, for the sake of the *Sādhaka* himself. The fact that the *Sādhaka* is not allowed to use a slave girl as his *Śakti* is significant in the sense that he should not force a woman to act as his *Śakti* in the ritual. In none of the above-mentioned texts there is any metioning of the *Śakti* belonging to the same religious system as the *Sādhaka*. Possibly this is self-evident and does not need to be stated explicitly, as is the case in, for instance, the *Kulārṇavatantra* (VII, 46d; 47b etc).

2. THE SĀDHAKA

Apart from the fact that the *Sādhaka* is very free in his choice of a *Śakti*, the *Sādhaka* himself is hardly bound by any restrictions. He is allowed to eat and drink to his liking, including liquors and meat—as is usual for a Tantric *Sādhaka*—since without it 'he should die in an instant' (III, 18cd; VI, 26; VII, 6cd; 7ab). He is permitted to accept food (MS E: money) from anyone (VII, 6ab; 7cd). There are no restrictions for the *Sādhana* regarding time of prayer, worship, etc.; there is no need for him to perform purifying rites for clothing, *āsana* etc.; for his *Sādhaka* no time is unsuited (VII, 11cd-14ab). The *Sādhaka* should, however, never ridicule a *Yoni*, nor should he show disgust nor shame (VI, 27ab). His behaviour towards women should not be offensive (VII, 14cd). *Maithuna* should only be performed by the *Sādhaka* for ritual purposes, never for worldly enjoyment in which case the *Sādhaka* is condemned to hell (V, 3).

It is obvious from the above lines that the *Yonitantra* permits a very free line of conduct on the part of the *Sādhaka*, who is dedicated to the *Yonipūjā*. He has the appearance of an ascetic, besmeared with mud or dirt (VII, 9ab), with unbound hairs and nude (II, 18c), but as his sole object is the *Yonipūjā* it excuses him from any other obligation.

3. TIME AND PLACE OF THE YONIPŪJĀ

Due to the very nature of the *Yonipūjā*, the most suitable time for the *Pūjā* is at night (II, 17d; 20d; 25d). The *Yonitantra* mentions some special occasions on which the *Yonipūjā* may be performed, thus assuring the *Sāahaka* of a particular result. When the *Sādhaka* should perform the ritual at the night of new moon—when all is dark—offering a *Bali* of rice boiled in milk with sugar and some ghee (*pāyasānna bali*) and a burned fish on a cross road, a cremation ground, or some other lonely spot, he is believed to acquire a great amount of wealth (II, 11cd-12cd). When the *Sādhaka* worships the *Yoni* during an eclipse of the sun or the moon, he will not be born again on earth again (III, 7cdff.). As to the place where the *Yonipūjā* should be performed, it is always some desolate spot hidden from the eyes of ther people: a cremation ground (II, 12a; VII, 5a; 19c), an empty house (II, 14d; VII, 22b), a closed-up house (II, 14d; VII, 5b; 22d), a *Liṅga* on a lonely spot (VII, 5c), etc.

According to the *Yonitantra* the *Yonipūjā* appears to be a completely private affair for the *Sādhaka*: it is not associated with any of the established festivals of Hindu society. The *Bṛhadyonitantra* (F. 3B), however, connects the *Yonipūjā* with the *Mahānavamī*, the last day of the *Durgāpūjā* in autumn.

3. THE CONCEPT BEHIND THE YONIPŪJĀ

Before dealing with the ritual itself, it might prove useful to examine the religious concept behind the *Yonipūjā* as seen in the *Yonitantra*. Unfortunately, the *Yonitantra* is not very elaborate on this point. The fact is stressed that the *Yonipūjā* is the worship *par excellence* (I, 5b; VI, 24cd), and by omitting it every other *Pūjā* is rendered worthless (VIII, 13). Any background for the importance of the *Yonipūjā* is not given, unless by such general remarks as that the Gods are born from the *Yoni* (I, 6), or that *Mahāmāyā* has the form of a *Yoni* and *Sadāśiva* the form of a *Liṅga* (V, 25ab; VI, 20ab). In the same context one should consider the remark that the *Guru* is Śiva and his wife the wife of Śiva (V, 3ab). In one instance (VIII, 4cd) the *Yonitantra* mentions the fact that especially in the *Kaliyuga* *Jaganmayī* has the form of the *Yoni*. The relation of the *Yoni* with the present *Kaliyuga* has been worked out more thoroughly in the *Samayācāratantra* (F. 11B), where we find the four *Yugas*, the four *Pīṭhas* and four parts of the body of the *Śakti* interrelated:

(1) *Pūrṇagiri* : *Kṛta-yuga* : the complete body of the *Śakti.*
(2) *Oḍiyāna* : *Tretā-yuga* : the head of the *Śakti.*
(3) *Jālandhara* : *Dvāpara-yuga* : the breasts of the *Śakti.*
(4) *Kāmapīṭha* : *Kali-yuga* : the *Yoni* of the *Śakti.*

The meaning of the above-sketched outline is, of course, that in the present age, the *Kaliyuga*, *Devī* is worshipped only with regard to Her *Yoni*, and that this worship takes place in the *Kāmapīṭha*, or Kāmarūpa.

The *Yoni* itself is sub-divided in the *Yonitantra* into ten parts (III, 14cdff.); each part being connected with a manifestation of *Devī*:

(1) *yonimūla* : *Devī* (MSS D, E, F: *Gaurī*)
(2) *yoni* : *Naganandinī*
(3) *yonicakra* : *Kālī*
(4) ,, : *Tārā*
(5) *yonikuntala* : *Chinnamastakā*
(6) *yonisamīpatas* : *Bagalā*
(7) ,, : *Mātaṅgī*
(8) *yonigarta* : *Mahālakṣmī*
(9) ,, : *Ṣoḍaśī*
(10) ,, : *Bhuvaneśvarī*

In *Paṭala* VIII, 8b-9a we find more or less the same Goddesses enumerated as manifestations of *Tripurā Kalī*: *Ṣoḍaśī*, *Bhuvaneśvarī*, *Chinnā*, *Tārā*, *Mahālakṣmī*, *Mātaṅgī*, *Kamalātmikā*, *Sundarī*, *Bhairavī*, and *Vidyā*. The names of the ten Goddesses in both lists are almost identical with those of the well-known '*Daśa Mahāvidyāḥ*.' which are most probably referred to in the *Yonitantra*.

The *Bṛhadyonitantra* (F. 2AB) deals more in detail with the concept behind the *Yonipūjā*. After explaining the triangular form (=*Yoni*) of *Mahāmāyā*/*Prakṛti* as the origin of the worlds, the Gods and the living beings, the *Bṛhadyonitantra* describes the *Yoni* in this context: in the three corners of the *Yoni* are Brahmā,

Viṣṇu and Maheśvara (=*sṛṣṭi, sthiti* and *saṃhāra*); on the right side of the triangle the river Yamunā flows, on the left side the Sarasvatī, and on the top the *Jāhnavī* (=the Ganges); in the centre of the triangle the abode of Kāmākhyā is situated, who is identified with *Kuṇḍalinī* and *Prakṛti* in the form of the menstrual flux (*puṣparūpiṇī*); the *Yoni* itself is Kāmarūpa, the *Yonipīṭha*. The *Bṛhadyonitantra* also sub-divides the *Yoni* into ten parts, connecting each part with one of the '*Daśa Mahāvidyāḥ*'. The different parts of the *Yoni*, however, bear other names than those found in the *Yonitantra*; the order and some of the names of the Goddesses likewise do not agree exactly with the two enumerations in the *Yonitantra*:

(1) *yonipārśva* : *Kālikā*
(2) ,, : *Tārā*
(3) *yonyūrdhva* : *Tripurasundarī*
(4) *yonimadhya* : *Bhuvaneśvarī*
(5) *yonimūla* : *Bhairavī*
(6) *yonigarta* : *Chinnamastā*
(7) *yonipränta* : *Dhūmā*
(8) *yoniromakūpa* : *Bagalā*
(9) *yonimekhalā* : *Mātaṅgī*
(10) *yonikṣetra* ; *Kamalā*.

The next point of interest with regard to the forms of *Devī* in connection with the *Yoni* is the mentioning of *Devī* as *Cāṇḍālī*: *yonimadhye pradhānā ca cāṇḍālī gaṇanāyikā* (*Yonitantra* III, 20ab). A *Cāṇḍālī* or *Caṇḍālī* belongs to one of the lowest groups of Hindu society, their main occupation being the execution of criminals and the transportation of the corpses of persons who do not have relatives (Manu X,51-56). It is a well-known fact that especially women living on the fringe of society were chosen as *Śakti* in the Tantric rituals. In *Vaiṣṇava Sahajiyā*, it was *Lokanātha Gosvāmi* who had a *Caṇḍāla* woman as his *Śakti* (Dimock, 1966, 216). In the *Kulārṇavatantra* (VII, 42a) a *Caṇḍālī* is among the eight so-called *Kula-śaktis*. Also in the Tantric and *Sahajiyā* literature of the Buddhists the *Caṇḍālī* appears to play an important role. In the Buddhist Tantras the *Caṇḍālī* more or less corresponds with the *Kuṇḍalinī*

Śakti of the Hindu Tantras (Dasgupta, 1964, 116ff.) In this aspect she appears evidently in the *Hevajratantra* (HT I, 1, 31). Furthermore, *Caṇḍālī* comes forward as one of a group of eight *yoginīs*—another being *Ḍombī*—surrounding *Hevajra* (HT I, 3, 10; II, 5, 33). In the Buddhist *Sahajiyā* songs the *Caṇḍālī* is mentioned throughout, together with the *Ḍombī*, another woman of low descent (cf: Dimock, 1966, 217).

So far, we have alluded several times to the *Vaiṣṇava* and Buddhist *Sahajiyā*. Although any direct relationship of the *Yonitantra* with the *Vaiṣṇava Sahajiyā* is not plausible due to the nature of the *Yonitantra* and the *Vaiṣṇava Sahajiyā* literature, one should keep in mind the following: the *Caṇḍālī* plays an important role in the *Vaiṣṇava Sahajiyā* literature, as well as in the *Yonitantra*—merely by worshipping a *Cāṇḍālī* the *Sādhaka* becomes *Śiva* Himself (*Yonitantra* III, 20). Furthermore, in the *Yonitantra Cāṇḍālī* is given the epithet *gaṇanāyikā* (III, 20b); although the term *Nāyikā* is common in Tantric literature it has a special connotation in *Vaiṣṇava Sahajiyā* literature, denoting a woman very suitable for the *Sahajiyā* ritual (Dimock, 1966, 215). The *Yonitantra* shows a preference for the *Śakti* not being the *Sādhaka's* own wife (VII, 17ab), which reminds us of the concept of *svakīya* and *parakīya* of the *Vaiṣṇava Sahajiyā* (cf: Dimock, 1966, 200ff.). Finally, we have suggested (vide: p. 17 supra) the *Vaiṣṇava Sahajiyā* literature to be a possible link between Viṣṇuism and Tantric literature.

Apart from these congruences with the *Vaiṣṇava Sahajiyā* literature in general, the mentioning of *Cāṇḍālī* in the *Yonitantra* might be due to another reason. According to the Petersburger Wörterbuch the name *Caṇḍālī* designates a woman on the first day of her menses—a fact of importance in the *Yonitantra*. In this context the connection with the *Bṛhadyonitantra* is evident, where in the centre of the *Yoni* the Goddess is given the epithet *puṣparūpiṇī* (vide: supra).

Besides these above-mentioned instances, the *Yonitantra* lacks any further information with regard to the background of the *Yonipūjā*. It seems sufficient for the *Yonitantra* to base its authority upon mythic events: the Pāṇḍavas became victorious in battle because they relied on the *Yoni* of Draupadī (IV, 28); Śiva conquered Death by it (I, 8), and destroyed the Tripura

(IV, 28); because Rāma worshipped the *Yoni* of Sītā, he was able to defeat Rāvaṇa and his family (IV, 7).

5. THE RITUAL OF THE YONIPŪJĀ

The basic ritual of the *Yonipūjā* is described in the first two *Paṭalas* of the *Yonitantra,* but only its main topics are dealt with. The exact ritual proceedings, *Bījas, Mantras,* etc., cannot be learned from the *Yonitantra.* The first *Paṭala* of the *Yonitantra* describes briefly the preliminary rites (I, 13cd-19ab) and the concluding ritual (I, 21cd-24) with an interlude (I, 19cd-21ab), giving the rules in case there is no *Guru* present at the time of the *Pūjā.* The central part of the ritual is again briefly referred to in the second *Paṭala* (II, 8-11ab).

The Preliminary Rites: The *Sādhaka* should procure a woman, who is wanton (*pramadā*), beloved (*kāntā*) and free from disgust or shame; she may either be his own beloved or someone else's. After having her placed, well clad, in the centre of the *Maṇḍala,* the *Sādhaka* should at first offer her *Vijayā,* some narcotic potion which is probably the modern *Bhāng* (cf: Avalon, 1972, 73 note 3). At this stage of the ritual the administration of a narcotic concoction is perfectly admissible being a part of the ritual itself; the *Sādhaka,* however, should not start the ritual with a woman in a drugged state as one might deduce from the *Bṛhadyonitantra* (F. 2B): *unmattāṃ nārcayed yoniṃ na paśyet sādhakottamaḥ.* Having placed the *Śakti* on his left thigh, the *Sādhaka* should honour her *Yoni* which is to be *sakuntalā,* not-shaven. In the *Yonitantra* as well as in the *Bṛhadyonitantra* (F. 2B), this condition of the *Yoni* is stressed upon; *na vinā kuntalāṃ yoniṃ mardayed...*(*Yonitantra* VI, 10ab). The reason for this particular condition of the *Yoni* is not explained neither in the *Yonitantra* nor in the *Bṛhadyonitantra,* but it certainly has a practical function in arousing the *Śakti* to a state of ecstasy (cf: *Yonitantra* II, 8ab). Moreover, the *Yonitantra* (V, 20) mentions the application of the pubic hair in some religious observances: should the *Sādhaka* take the hairs of the *Yoni* to *Rājagṛha,* all his (religious) undertakings will prove successful. A possible explanation, however, for the importance laid upon the pubic hair, might be inferred from the *Bṛhadāraṇyaka Upaniṣad* (VI, 4, 3), where the pubic hair of the *Yoni* is identified with the layer of *Kuśa* grass (*barhis*) in Vedic ritual. The next step in the ritual of the *Yonipūjā* as desribed in the *Yonitantra*, consists of the anointment of the *Yonigarta* with Sandal paste (*candana*) to let it look like a 'ravishing flower' (I, 15cd). After this the *Sādhaka* gives his *Śakti* wine (*kāraṇa*) to drink and he paints an *Ardhacandra* on her forehead with vermilion (*sindūra*). Next, the *Sādhaka* places his hands on her breasts and mutters the *Bhagabīja* (?) between them. The *Yonitantra* does not explain what the *Sādhaka* mutters at this point, but probably he mutters the *Bhagabīja* 108 times, to which the *Bṛhadyonitantra* (F. 5A) seems to point at this stage of the ritual. The *Bhaga*-or *Yonibīja* is given in the *Bṛhadyonitantra* (F. 6B) in a concealed way, but unfortunately the lines are rather corrupt; probably the *Bhagabīja* is identical with the *Māyābīja*, *HRĪM*, here. Apparently to bring the *Śakti* in a state of sexual excitement, the *Sādhaka* kisses her on the cheeks (BYT F. 5B: mouth), and moulds her breasts. The concluding part of the preliminary rites is the recitation of the *Mahāmanu* (=*Bhagabīja* ?) 108 or a thousand times over the *Yoni*, and the recitation of a *Stotra*. Again, the *Yonitantra* is vague leaving the nature of this *Stotra* unexplained, but most probably it is the *Tryambakamantra* (VS III, 60) which is uttered in the *Bṛhadyonitantra* (F. 5A) at the time of inserting the *Liṅga* into the *Yoni*, this being the next step in the ritual of the *Yonipūjā*.

Just as the *Yoni* is anointed with Sandal paste, likewise the *Liṅga* is anointed with Sandal paste and Saffran (*kuṅkuma*) by the *Śakti* (II, 9).

The Central Ritual: The basic part of the *Yonipūjā* is formed by ritual coition. The object of the performance of this ritual coition is the production of the fluid called *Tattva Uttama*, 'The Sublime Essence', or *Yonitattva*.

The Concluding Rites: To conclude the ritual the *Sādhaka* should pay his respects both to the *Yonimaṇḍala* and the *Guru*. Finally, *the Sādhaka* utters some lines (I, 23-24) expressing that he has accomplished his purpose by which he has been saved from the *Narakārṇava*, the Hellish Sea (=*the Saṃsāra*).

As it is evident from the preceding lines, the ritual performed in order to gain the *Yonitattva* is a rather simple affair according to the *Yonitantra*. The *Bṛhadyonitantra*, on the other hand, is far more detailed. We have already seen that we had to turn to the *Bṛhadyonitantra* in order to learn the *Bījas* and *Mantras* of the ritual. Furthermore, the *Yonitantra* refers in one instance (III,13c) to the *Kavaca* (*-mantra*), but it does not give any particulars. The *Bṛhadyonitantra* (F. 9Aff.), however, deals at length with the *Yonikavaca* which is given in full. Most likely, the *Yonikavacamantra* of the *Bṛhadyonitantra* is meant by the *Yonitantra*: in both texts the *Sādhaka* is said to become a *Kālikāputra* by recitation of this particular *Mantra* (*Yonitantra* II, 14a; BYT F.8B). The *Yonitantra* uses five times the term *Mahāyoni* (I, 24a; II, 23a; III, 5c; 23; VII, 29a). It remains obscure, however, what exactly is meant by this designation. The *Bṛhadyonitantra* mentions the *Mahāyoni* only once (F.5A) in the description of the ritual of the *Yonipūjā*. It seems, that here the term *Mahāyoni* is a designation for the *Śakti* or her *Yoni* at a certain phase of the ritual: when the Goddesses who actually are manifestations of the *Yoni*, are duly worshipped, the *Yoni* of the *Śakti* becomes designated as *Mahāyoni*, the *Yoni* of *Devī* Herself. The names of these Goddesses are mentioned in the *Bṛhadyonitantra* (F.5A) : *Bhagā*, *Bhagākṣī Bhagajihvikā* (cf : KP LXI ,113; 114: LXIII, 102; 103): Finally, in the *Bṛhadyonitantra* the ritual of the *Yonipūjā* is connected with the Six *Cakras* (FF. 9Aff.) since *Kuṇḍalinī* is stated to be the personification of the *Yoni* (BYT F.6B). The *Yonitantra* does not mention on any occasion even one of the Six *Cakras*, a fact which is rather remarkable for a text calling itself a *Tantra*.

As we have seen, the main purpose for performing the *Yonipūjā* in that *Yonitantra* is the production of the *Yonitattva*. The *Yonitantra* nor the *Bṛhadyonitantra* explain how the *Sādhaka* is supposed to extract this *Yonitattva* from the *Yoni* of his *Śakti*. Probably this is accomplished by means of the *Vajrolīmudrā* (cf: HYP III, 82-89; ŚS IV, 52ff.; Lorenzen, 1972, 91). This *Yonitattva* has a twofold application: the *Sādhaka* can either make himself a *Tilaka* with it, or he can worship *Devī* with it in Her *Yoni*-form. The *Yonitantra* prescribes the *Yonipūjā* to be performed every day (II, 6ab; IV,30a) to enable the *Sādhaka* to make his—daily—*Tilaka* by means of the *Yonitattva*

(V, 4cd; VII, 21). On special occasions, the *Tilaka* made with the *Yonitattva* may even render the *Sādhaka* victorious in battle (VI, 6cd; 7ab) as it did the *Pāṇḍavas* (IV, 28cd); in combination with gold this *Tilaka* secures the *Sādhaka's* glorification in the *Durgāloka* (V, 21). The second application of the *Yonitattva*, viz. to worship *Śakti/Devī*, is described in *Paṭala* II, 22ff: the *Sādhaka* worships the *Mahāyoni* with water used for cleansing the *Yoni* and the *Liṅga*; next he offers *Arghya* consisting of *Yonitattva*[7] to Her. This is divided into three parts: one part the *Sādhaka* presents to the *Śakti/Devī*, the other two parts the *Sādhaka* drinks himself, mixed with wine. The consuming of the *Yonitattva* by the *Sādhaka*, we know also from other sources: the *Mātṛkābhedatantra* (V, 34ff.), for instance, gives a prescription for a concoction based on *Yonitattva*, or more precisely *Yonipuṣpa* (vide sub), which ensures the virility of the *Sādhaka* after drinking it: *pratyahaṃ parameśāni śatanarīṃ ramed yadi/vīryādirahitaṃ na syāt tejovṛddhikaraṃ param* (*Mātṛkābhedatantra* V, 40).

The consuming of the *Yonitattva*, whether symbolically or actually performed, has not been accounted for in the *Yonitantra*. The concept on which it is based, however, we can learn from other sources dealing with the same subject: The *Bindu* is the cause (*mūla*) of the human body (GŚ 68); it is twofold: pale-white (*pāṇḍura*) and blood-red (*lohita*); the former being the semen virile, the latter the menstrual fluid (GŚ 72). The two are identified with *Śiva/Candra* and *Śakti/Sūrya* respectively (GŚ 73; 74; ŚS IV, 58; 59). Uniting these two the *Sādhaka* attains the highest state (GŚ 74). Since the *Bindu* is the root of the body it is essential to keep it in the body (ŚS IV, 58), by loss of the *Bindu* death is inevitable, but by preserving it the *Sādhaka* overcomes death (GŚ 70; ŚS IV, 61; HYP III, 87). In this context may be placed *Yonitantra* I, 8ab: *ahaṃ mṛtyuṃjayo devi tava Yoniprasādataḥ*. The place of origin of the *Bindu* is believed to be situated above the throat, from where it oozes down. To keep the *Bindu* in his body, the *Sādhaka* closes the aperture above his throat by means of the *Khecarīmudrā* thus

[7]In II, 23c *toyam* is undoubtedly a synonym for (*Yoni-*) *tattva*, as MS D reads. The ST (F.108) has the same meaning of *toyam*.

preventing the *Bindu* from going downwards (GŚ 69). In the *Yonitantra* no mention is made of this *Khecarīmudra*. Here, the *Bindu* is kept in the body by simply consuming it when discharged.

Dasqupta (1946, 287) has already hinted at the similarity between the drinking of the Vedic *Soma*-juice and the consumption of the *Yonitattva*. Besides the connection between *Soma* and the *Bindu* based on their mutual identification with the moon, on which Dasgupta bases his argument, a more striking similarity is found. *Soma* is described as being of a reddish colour (*aruṇá, aruṣá, babhrú*), or golden like the sun (ṚgS I, 46, 10ab); in this aspect the *Soma* may easily be compared with the menstrual flux in the Tantric *Sādhana*. To render the pure *Soma*-juice fit for consumption, it is diluted with milk or water. *Soma*-juice mixed with milk is described as having a whitish colour (ṚgS IV, 27, 5a: IX, 74, 7a): both, the milk and the whitish mixture, are in the Tantric conception comparable with the white semen virile added to the red menstrual flux. Furthermore, milk and water are both identified with semen (*rétas*) in Vedic literature (ŚB IX, 5, 1, 56; III, 8, 4, 11). Likewise, the *Soma* itself is compared with the semen of a stallion (ṚgS I, 164, 35c). Evidently, the Tantric *Sādhaka* finds ample grounds for an identification of the *Yonitattva* with the Vedic *Soma*-juice. In the Tantric conception the Vedic *Soma*-juice mixed with milk or water has been equalized with *Yonitattva*, the union of seminal and ovarian fluids. The Tantric *Sādhaka*, however, carries the comparison even further: just as the pure *Soma*-juice is mixed with milk or water, likewise the *Sādhaka* mixes—again—the *Yonitattva* with wine (*Yonitantra* II, 24b) or with water (ST F. 10B). Although it is apparent that the Vedic drinking of the *Soma* has been transformed into a yogic practice connected with the *Yonitattva*, the *Tantras* do not mention this relation explicitly due to their general repugnance to the Vedic sacrificial institution.

A special occasion for the application of the *Yonitattva* is mentioned in the *Yonitantra* during the *Śrāddha*-ritual. In *Paṭala* V, 5cd-7ab the *Yonitantra* recommends the attendance of *Kaula vipras* during the Śrāddha ceremony in order to secure a heavenly abode for the *Pitaras* of the *Sādhaka*. Although at this instance no mentioning is made of the *Yonitattva*, it is nevertheless implied as we learn from *Yonitantra* VII, 28ab; 'Due to *Tarpāṇa* with *Yonittattva* the *Pitaras* hold a heavenly abode'.

As we have mentioned earlier, the ritual coition with a woman during her monthly periods is recommended in the *Yonitantra.* Although much abhorred in Hindu society, the fact itself is certainly not unknown in mythology and in reality. The birth of the *Asura* Naraka (vide supra) is the result of this kind of sexual union: Viṣṇu in His Boar-*avatāra* enjoyed sexual intercourse with the Earth during Her monthly periods; out of this union Naraka was born (cf: KP XXXVI, 1ff.) The birth of Naraka is a mythic event in its true sense, since progeny under these conditions is highly improbable unless it is *Asura* progeny. The modern Bauls of Bengal do know a similar *Sādhana,* to which Capwell (1974, 262) smartly remarks, "A notable characteristic of Baul families is their smallness; many have no children, others have them only as 'accidents', the result of imperfectly performed sadhana...". This implication of coition with a woman during her *menses,* reminds strongly of the condition of the *Śakti* in the *Yonitantra,* who should be childless (vide supra).

In the *Yonitantra* the menstrual flux is designated with the term 'flower' (*puṣpa*), a common designation for it in *Sanskrit.* Again, the *Yonitantra* shows a tendency towards superficiality. In their effort to rubricate everything, the Indians discern at least six types of the menstrual flux: *svayaṃbhū-*, *kuṇḍagola-*, *sva-*, *vajra-*, and *sarvakālodbhava-puṣpa* (*Mātṛkābhedatantra* V, 27-33). The *Yonitantra* makes only use of the general designation *puṣpa,* except perhaps in *Paṭala* III, 13b where *svapuṣpa* is mentioned. In view of the fact, however, that this is the only occurrence of the word, it remains doubtful whether *svapuṣpa* is used in its technical sense: the first menstrual blood of a girl after her marriage (*Mātṛkābhedatantra* V, 31). Moreover, the above-mentioned place in the *Yonitantra* seems only to deal with wine as a substitute for the *Sādhaka's* semen mixed with the menstrual blood of the *Śakti.*

Resuming, we find in the *Yonitantra* two kinds of the 'Sublime Essence': the *Yonitattva* and the *Yonipuṣpa.* The application of both types is much the same, although the *Yonipuṣpa* is perhaps held in higher esteem leading, for instance, directly towards *Mokṣa* (I,12cd; 13ab). The anointment of the *Yoni* with the red Sandal paste to let it look like a *puṣpa manohara* (I,15cd), may be based upon this superiority of *Yoni* during the menses of a *Śakti*.

In connection with the application of the menstrual blood in worshipping *Devī*, it is useful to mention the so-called *Devatāsnāna* as described in the *Samayācāratantra* (FF. 10AB): mixed with water in a copper plate, it is used to bath the statues of Divinities. The *Samayācāratantra*, however, mentions at least three out of the six different kinds of 'flowers' (*svayaṃbhū-*, *kuṇḍa-*, *gola-puṣpa*).

VII. EVALUATION OF THE YONITANTRA

Reviewing the previous sections, we may end this introduction with the following remarks. The *Yonitantra* had its origin in the region of Cooch Bihar and can be placed in a *Vaiṣṇava* environment around the worship of the Goddess Mādhavī. This Mādhavī may be regarded as the *Vaiṣṇava* counterpart of the *Śaiva* Kāmākhyā in Kāmarūpa. The *Yonitantra* seeks to surpass its *Vaiṣṇava* limitations by allying itself with the *Kulācāra*, thus trying to find a more general acknowledgement beyond the boundaries of 'Sectarianism'. In this context one should place the conspicuous absence of any direct reference to Kāmākhyā or Kāmarūpa. Furthermore, the superficiality of the *Yonitantra* should be mentioned with regard to the *Śakti*, the *Śadhaka* and the ritual itself, comparing the *Yonitantra* with other texts dealing with the same subject.

Returning to the very beginning of this introduction, the remark of Briggs seems now hardly applicable to the *Yonitantra* in its present edition. We have seen that the *Bṛhadyonitantra* deals in far more detail with the ritual of the *Yonipūjā*, especially giving it an ample religious background. One could therefore decide in favour of the BYT for occupying a place next to the *Mahānirvāṇatantra* and the *Kālikāpurāṇa*. Unfortunately, no critically evaluated text of Bṛhadyonitantra is available. However, both texts, the *Yonitantra* and the *Bṛhadyonitantra*, are rather insignificant compared with the *Mahānirvāṇatantra* and the *Kālikāpurāṇa*, with regard to their contents and size. Most probably Briggs had the *Yoginītantra* in mind, which is a very distinct glorification of *Kāmākhyā* and *Kāmarūpa*, much more so than the *Yonitantra* and the *Bṛhadyonitantra*. Moreover, the *Yonitantra* and the *Yoginītantra* are sometimes mistaken for each other, as we will see in Part II.

Although the *Yonitantra* is not likely to occupy the place attributed to it by Briggs, the text is important by itself. It provides us with information on that side of Tantric *Sādhana* which is only hinted at in the texts, but which has remained virtually unknown.

THE YONITANTRA

PART II: TEXT

Introduction

THE MANUSCRIPTS

FOR OUR critical edition of the *Yonitantra* we have used the following six MSS:

A: MS No. 6088 in the collections of the RASB.
Substance, country-made paper. $7\frac{1}{2} \times 4\frac{3}{4}$ inches. Folia, 25. Lines, 7 on a page. Extent in *Ślokas*, 255. Character, modern Kashmiri. Appearance, fresh. Complete in eight chapters.

B: MS No. 2889 in the collections of the RASB.
Substance, country-made yellow papea. 15×4 inches. Folia, 17. Lines, 5 on a page. Extent in *Ślokas*, 250. Character, Bengali. Appearance, fresh. Complete in eight chapters.

C: MS No. 4672 in the collections of the RASB.
Substance, country-made paper. 14×5 inches. Folia, 8. Lines, 9 on a page. Extent in *Ślokas*, 200, Chapter, Bengali. Appearance, old and discoloured. Complete in eight chapters.

D: MS No. 5093 in the collections of the RASB.
Substance, country-made paper, $14\frac{1}{2} \times 4$ inches. Folia, 9. Lines, 8 on a page. Extent in *Ślokas*, 225. Character, Bengali. Appearance, old and discoloured. Complete in eight chapters.

Since we had only the microfilms of the MSS at our disposal, we rely on their description as given in the 'Descriptive Catalogue of the Sanskrit Manuscripts in the collections of the Royal Asiatic Society of Bengal' (Calcutta, 1939, Volume VIII, part I). According to the catalogue MS B is described in 'Notices of Sanskrit Manuscripts' (First Series, Volume X, Part I, 3185) by

Rājendralāl Mitra (Calcutta, 1892). Unfortunately we had no opportunity to consult this description.

E: MS No. 1946 in the collection of the Baṅgīya Sāhitya Pariṣad (Calcutta). Substance, country-made paper. Folia, 9. Lines, 8 on a page. Character, Bengali. Complete in eight chapters.

F: MS No. 1388 in the collection of the Baṅgīya Sāhitya Pariṣad (Calcutta). Substance, country-made paper. Folia, 13. Lines, 7 on a page. Character, Bengali. Complete in eight chapters.

The two MSS of the Baṅgīya Sāhitya Pariṣad have not been described in any catalogue. The MSS are probably written on country-made paper, as far as we could discern from the microfilms.

To our knowledge there exist only two other MSS of the *Yonitnatra* which were, however, inaccessible to us. They are included in the '*Descriptive Catalogue of Sanskrit Manuscripts of Orissa*' (Volume V) compiled by Sri Mahesh Prasad Dash, curator of the Orissa State Museum (Bhubaneswar, 1965). As far as the text of the two MSS is reproduced in the catalogue, they show some variant readings not accounted for in the MSS we have used. The first MS (No.T/35(b)) is written on palm-leaf in Oriyan script; it is complete in eight chapters, and was probably written in the 18th century according to the catalogue. The second MS (No. T/9(c)) is also written on palm-leaf in Oriyan script. It is, however, incomplete: the last *Paṭala* is omitted. According to Sri Mahesh Prasad Dash it was written in the 18th century. The most significant fact with regard to this second MS is its title. In the catalogue this MS is called *Yoginītantra*, a name given by the text itself (*iti Yoginitantre prathamaḥ paṭalaḥ*, etc.). From the lines quoted in the catalogue, however, it becomes evident that the text is actually the *Yonitantra*, and not the *Yoginītantra*. We assumed earlier (p. 33) that Briggs mistook the *Yonitantra* for the *Yoginītantra*; here we see the reverse: the *Yoginītantra* is mistaken for the *Yonitantra*. Obviouly, the two texts are easily confused with regard to their names.
Leaving aside the two Oriyan MSS, the following remarks can

be made with regard to the MSS we have used for our critical edition of the *Yonitantra*. All the MSS are complete in eight chapters, although the number of *Ślokas* differs. The omission of lines seems to be an individual affair for the MSS. Some remarks, however, should be made. MS C omits I, 19cd-21cd, which is evidently an interlude. The passage dealing with the *Kulamāhātmya* (*paṭala* IV) is for its major part omitted in MS A. Since this passage seems to be influenced by the second *Ullāsa* of the *Kulārṇavatantra*, one might assume that the author of MS A—the only MS not written in Bengali script—was not acquainted with that text. MS B omits in *Paṭala* V most of the lines dealing with the *Śrāddha*-ritual, but does include the other reference in the text to this ritual (VII, 28ab).

Among the MSS two related groups can be discerned:

(I) MSS B & E: Both MSS show often similar readings, or readings with the same purport, differing from the other MSS. Thus, III, 2b *vadhabandhanam* (B: *maraṇaṃ dhruvam*; E: *mṛtyur eva ca*); IV, 10a *ahaṃ viṣṇuś ca brahmā* (B,E: *ahaṃ brahmā ca viṣṇuś*); IV, 28b *nihataṃ* (B,E: *hatavān*); in *paṭala* V both MSS omit 23ab-24ab.

(II) MSS D & F: Both MSS choose in their readings often for a Lectio Facilior. Thus, II 7d *pūjanaṃ ca kutobhayam* (D: *pūjāṃ cāpi kulocitāṃ*; F: *pūjāṃ cāpi kulodbhavām*); II. 20b *caturvargaṃ labhen naraḥ* (D,F; *caturvargaphalaṃ labhet*); V, 13d *samācaret* (D,F: *karoti yaḥ*); V, 18b *samācaret* (D,F: *karoti ca*); instead of *susama* (V, 28d; VI, 6a;15a) both MSS read *sugama*.

The MSS A & C cannot be related definitely with any of the other MSS; both appear to occupy a rather solitary place among the MSS used for the critical edition of the *Yonitantra*. MS A distinguishes oneself from all the other MSS by the fact that it is the only MS not written in Bengali script, and that it has a completely different order of *Ślokas* in the second chapter. Sometimes the readings of MS A differ considerably from those of the other MSS (cf: IV, 19c; V, 5c).

THE TEXT

As is evident at first sight, the text of the *Yonitantra* is written in a rather simple Sanskrit not claiming any literary merit. The few lines written in a more elegant or difficult style, appear to have been borrowed from other texts (II, 5cd; 18cd; IV, 14cd; cf: Appendix). Related to the simple style of the *Yonitantra*, is the fact that a considerable number of *Pādas* are repeated throughout the text with only slight modifications. The *Pāda muktaḥ koṭikulaiḥ saha* is found five times (II,14b; IV, 25d; V, 9b; VII, 3d; 29d); its variant *tadā kotikulaiḥ sākam* is found in II, 22a. The *Pāda . . . janmārjitaṃ pāpam* is accounted for in four instances, with a different first part each time (III, 12c; VI, 25c; VII, 21c; 29c). The *Pāda pañcatattvam vinā devi/durge* occurs five times (III, 10a; IV, 12a; V,16a; VI, 31c; VII, 24c). It is in four instances followed either by the *Pāda sarvaṃ ca niṣphalaṃ bhavet* or its variants, or by the *Pāda . . . vṛthā bhavet* with the same connotation. Likewise *Pādas* as *yonipūjām vinā durge* (III, 19c; 21c), *yoniṃ vinā maheśāni* (VIII,13a;14a) and *bhagaṃ vinā maheśāni* (VII, 27a) follow the same pattern, being followed by either of the two *Pādas* mentioned above. *Pādas* containing a compound ending on-*mātreṇa* are frequently used (II, 6c; III, 7a; 20e; IV, 6a; 17b; V, 3c: 25c; VI, 4c; VII, 3a; 27c: VIII, 6c). *Pādas* ending on *puraskṛtya/upāsyaiva* with as their first part an Accusative are five times met with (I, 7a;10c; III, 5a; V,1a; 13c). The *Pāda tilakaṃ yonitattvena/-puṣpena* is found four times (II,7a; IV,18c; V,4c;21a). For a text as short as the *Yonitantra*, the total number of repetitions and close variants seems to be rather high.

The *Yonitantra* is composed in the *Śloka* metre, which is applied regularly. Only in III, 13a (*retoyuktena puṣpena*) the variant reading *retayuktena puṣpena* (MSS B, D) furnishes a smoother rhythm.

Three *Pādas* have an irregular number of syllables. In *Paṭala* I, 6a we find nine syllables (*hariharādyāś ca ye devāḥ*); only the MSS A and E have the prescribed eight syllables (A : *harer ādyāś ca ye devāḥ*; E: *hariharādyā ye devāḥ*), but the latter has been 'corrected' again into nine syllables (E^1). *Pāda* 12c of the third *Paṭala* (*ayuta Pjanmārjitaṃ pāpaṃ*) has also nine syllables, but here the problem is solved by ignoring the *Daṇḍa* at the end of the previous *Pāda*: . . . *yady* (/) *ayuta-* . . . Although the MSS A, B, E have the regular number of eight syllables (A: *yutaṃ janmā-* . . . ; B; *saptajamnā* . . .; E: *yāvad janmā-* . . .), the reading *ayuta-* seems to be correct, since in the previous *Pāda* the same number *-ayuta-* is mentioned. To ignore the *Daṇḍa* between *Pādas* is easily understandable, since the *Daṇḍa* is often not written in the MSS. The same tendency (viz. to ignore the *Daṇḍa*) we see in I, 17bc (. . . *kucopari/aṣṭottara-* . . .). Two MSS seem to insert a hiatus-filler; A: . . . *kucopari*(/)*tatrāṣṭottara-*. . ., and D: ... *kucopari* (/) *cāṣṭottara-*.... In *Paṭala* V *Pāda* 29b has only seven syllables ('*bhaktebhyo viṣeṣataḥ*) due to *Sandhi*. The MSS A[1], & F have a *Lectio Facilior* (*nābhaktebhyo viśeṣataḥ*) resulting in the required eight syllables. We should, however, accept hiatus at the caesura, which is not unknown in our text. Thus, . . . *paraśi-ṣyebhyo, abhaktebhyo viśeṣataḥ*.

Hiatus between the first and second, third and fourth *Pādas* (i.e. the caesura) of a *Śloka* seems to be an accepted feature in the *Yonitantra*. We have noted thirteen such cases (I,3ab (D corrects); III,10cd; 25cd etc.). Hiatus occurs thrice inside a *Pāda* (I,8d; V,24c; VIII,8a). *Sandhi* is ignored unanimously in all the MSS in I,21c (*pūjāvasāne āgatya*). On one occasion the caesura is ignored (II,2ab: *saṃkṣepāt kathitā yonipūjāvidhir anuttamā*).

There are only a few cases in the text, where an emendation seems to be called for. In *Paṭala* II,llc all the MSS read *bhaumāvasyām* or *bhaumāvāsyām*, but to our knowledge this form is not accounted for in any text, so far. The form *bhaumā-vāsyām* might, however, be understood as a contraction of *bhauma* (*-vāra*) and *amāvāsyām*, which seems not too unlikely in view of the fact that in *Śloka* 13a *bhaumavāra* is mentioned. We have, however, emended to *amāvāsyāṃ*. In *Pāda* 13a of the same *Paṭala* we have emended the reading *citāyāṃ* of all the MSS into the more probable *citrāyāṃ*. In *Paṭala* IV,16d we have chosen for the Vocative, which none of the MSS reads, although the Nominative (MSS B,D,E,F,) is understandable: 'O Best of the *Sādhakas*, come hither; I am devoted to the worship of the *Yoni*'. With reference to VII,30a (*śiṣyānāṃ kanyakāyoniṃ*) we have emended IV,29d into *śiṣyānāṃ yonim*.... In *Paṭala* VI, 5b we read *sampūjyaś*, which might be meant by the MSS B & C (*sampūjya*); the reading of MS F (*pūjyate*) is evidently a *Lectio Facilior*. In the same *Paṭala* the reading of all the MSS for *Śloka* 16ab (. . .*mahādeva, saṃśayo*. . .) is emended into. . .*mahādevāsaṃśayo* . . ., which gives a better understanding of the text, although in doing so the caesura is ignored.

As becomes evident from the variant readings, the authors of the MSS tried to write grammatically correct Sanskrit, in which they have succeeded to some extent. Perhaps one remark should be made in connection with the gender and the declension of the word *vidhi*. The word *vidhi* occurs fours times: thrice as the last part of the compound *yonipūjāvidhi* (I,23a; II,2b; IV, ld) and once on its own (V,22a). The MSS do not agree upon the gender of the word, which should be masculine, though. We have chosen for the feminine gender, however, which is accounted for in the MSS. The main reason to accept the feminine gender for the word *vidhi* is found in *Paṭala* V, 22a. Five out of the six MSS read *vidhā* (A,B,C,E,F,), which is evidently meant as an Instrumental Singular. Although *vidhā* might be the Instrumental Singular of a word *vidh*, more probably it is a corruption of *vidhyā* the Instrumental Singular of a feminine I-stem. Moreover, the reading *vidhinā* (MS D) result in nine syllables for the *Pāda*. Only MS B takes the consequence of the feminine gender of *vidhi*, and reads *kayā* (A,C,D,E,F: *kena*). Although the form *vidhyā* is accounted for in Vedic Sanskrit as a masculine Instrumental Singular, this seems hardly the case in the *Yonitantra*. We have accepted the feminine gender of the word *vidhi* in view of the fact that especially in the case of I-stems confusion of gender is not unlikely.

In the critical presentation we have included those variant readings which provide a notably different reading of the text. Since we have assumed that that the *Yonitantra* was written in grammatically correct Sanskrit, or at least that the effort was made to do so, we have excluded most of the cases of obvious carelessness towards *Sandhi* etc. Furthermore, the MSS C and D show a certain tendency towards 'untidiness', often forgetting one or more syllables; most of these cases have not been included in this edition.

THE YONITANTRA

Yonitantra, Paṭala 1

(1) [0]kailāsaśikharārūḍhaṃ devadevam jagadgurum /
sadāsmeramukhī durgā[1] papraccha[2] naganandinī[3] //[4]
(2) catuḥṣaṣṭīni[5] tantrāṇi[5] kṛtāni bhavatā prabho /
teṣāṃ madhye pradhānāni[6] vada me karuṇānidhe //
mahādeva[7] uvāca //
(3) śṛṇu pārvati cārvaṅgi asti[8] guhyatamaṃ priye /
koṭivāraṃ vāritāsi[9] tathāpi śrotum icchasi //
(4) strīsvabhāvāc[10] ca[11] cārvaṅgi[12] śaśvān[13] māṃ paripṛcchasi[14] / [15]
gopanīyaṃ prayatnena tvayaiva[16] vidyate[16] ca[16] tat[16] //
(5) mantrapīṭhaṃ[17] yantrapīṭhaṃ[18] yonipīṭhaṃ ca[19] pārvati[19] /
yonipīṭhaṃ pradhānaṃ hi tava snehāt prakāśyate //[20]
(6) hariharādyāś[21] ca[21] ye devāḥ sṛṣṭisthityantakārakāḥ [22] / [23]
sarve vai yonisaṃbhūtāḥ śṛṇuṣva naganandini // [24]
(7) śaktimantram upāsyaiva yadi yoniṃ na[25] pūjayet[25] /
teṣāṃ dīkṣā[23] ca mantraś[26] ca narakāyopapadyate //
(8) ahaṃ mṛtyuṃjayo devi tava yoniprasādataḥ / [27]
tava yoniṃ mahādevi[28] bhāvayāmi[29] aharniśam //
(9) pūjayāmi sadā durge hṛtpadme[30] surasundari [31] /
divyabhāvo vīrabhāvo yasya citte virājate //
(10) anāyāsena deveśi tasya[32] muktiḥ[32] kare sthitā /
śaktimantraṃ puraskṛtya yo[33] vā[33] yoniprapūjakaḥ [34] //
(11) sa dhanyaḥ sa[35] kavir[35] dhīmān sarvajño[36] 'pi surāsuraiḥ /
brahmā yadi caturvaktraḥ[37] kalpakoṭiśatair api //
(12) tadā[38] vaktuṃ na śaknoti[39] kim anyair bahubhāṣitaiḥ /
yadi bhāgyavaśenāpi sapuṣpāṃ[40] milate[41] ca[42] tām[42] //

(13) tadaiva[43] mahatīṃ pūjāṃ kṛtvā mokṣam avāpnuyāt/
ānīya pramadāṃ kāntāṃ ghṛṇālajjāvivarjitām //
(14) svakāntāṃ parakāntāṃ vā suveśāṃ sthāpya maṇḍale/
prathame[44] vijayāṃ[45] datvā[46] pūjayed bhaktibhāvataḥ //
(15) vāmorau[47] tāṃ[48] ca[48] saṃsthāpya[48] yajed[49] yoniṃ[50] sakuntalām[50] /
yonigarte[51] candanaṃ ca dadyāt puṣpaṃ manoharam //
(16) tatra cāvāhanaṃ nāsti jīvanyāsaṃ tathā[52] manuḥ[52] /
tanmukhe kāraṇaṃ datvā[53] sindūreṇārdhacandrakam //
(17) lalāṭe candanaṃ datvā hastadvayaṃ kucopari /
aṣṭottaraśataṃ[54] japtvā stanamadhye[55] varānane //
(18) kucayor[56] mardanaṃ[56] kuryād[56] gaṇḍacumbanapūrvakam /
aṣṭottaraśataṃ vāpi sahasram yonimaṇḍale //
(19) japtvā mahāmanuṃ[57] stotraṃ[57] paṭhed bhaktiparāyaṇaḥ /
pūjākāle[58] gurur[58] na[58] syāt[58] tatra[59] sādhaka[60] uttamaḥ[60] // [61]
(20) pūjako 'haṃ[62] svayaṃ tatra[63] nātra kāryā vicaraṇā / [64]
guror agre pṛthakpūjā viphalā ca na saṃśayaḥ // [65]
(21) tasmād[66] bahutarair[66] yatnair[66] gurave ca samarpayet / [67]
pūjāvasāne āgatya praṇamed yonimaṇḍalam[68] // [69]
(22) puṣpāñjalitrayaṃ datvā[70] svaguruṃ[71] praṇamet punaḥ [72] /
prārthayed bahuyatnena kṛtāñjalipuṭaḥ sudhīḥ [73] //
(23) yonipūjāvidhiṃ kṛtvā[74] kṛtārtho 'smi na saṃśayaḥ /
adya me saphalam janma jīvitam[75] ca sujīvitam //
(24) pūjām kṛtvā mahāyonim[76] uddhṛto[77] narakārṇavāt //

ti yonitantre prathamaḥ paṭalaḥ // [78]

Yonitantra, Paṭala 1: Variant Readings

o OṂ namo bhavānyai : A; OṂ namaḥ śrīgurave: B; OṂ namaḥ parama ( ) vatāyai: C; ( ) namaḥ: D; OṂ namaḥ Kālikāyai: E; omitted by F.

[1]devī: C.

[2]pṛcchati: A.

[3]parameśvaram: B.
[4]After Śloka 1cd B inserts: śrīdevy uvāca.
[5]-ṣaṣṭi tantra yāni:=A;- ṣaṣṭiś ca tantrāṇi: C, E.
[6]pradhānāṃ hi: B.
[7]śrīmahādeva: F; īśvara: A, D.
[8]cāsti: D.
[9]kathitāsi: E.
[10]-bhāvā: C; -bhāvād: A.
[11]dhi: A; Omitted by C.
[12]cārvaṅgī: F.
[13]śvan: F; tathā: C.
[14]pṛcchasi: A.
[15]Śloka 4ab omitted by E.
[16]tvayy avavidyate ca tat: C; tavyy eva vidyate ca tat: F; priyeṇa vidyate tataḥ: B; na prakāśyaṃ kadācana: E; D is illegible.
[17]yantrapīṭhaṃ: D, F.
[18]manaḥpīṭham D; liṅgapīṭham: F.
[19]śṛṇuṣva tat: D.
[20]Śloka 5cd omitted by D.
[21]hariharādyā: E. (E[1]: hariharādhyāś ca); harer ādyāś ca: A.
[22]-kāriṇaḥ: A.
[23]Śloka 6ab omitted by D.
[24]Śloka 6cd omitted by D.
[25]prapūjayet: C.
[26]dīkṣāś ca mantrāś: C.
[27]Śloka 8b omitted by E.
[28]maheśāni: A; bhāvayāmi: B; Śloka 8c omitted by E.
[29]mahādevi: B.
[30]hṛtpadmeṣu: A; japāmi: D.
[31]ca sundari: A, ca sureśvari: F.
[32]muktis tasya: D.
[33]yāvad: E.
[34]yonim pra-: E; yoniḥ pra-: B.
[35]sādhako: E.
[36]sa mānyo: E.
[37]-vaktraiḥ: A, D.
[38]tad: E.
[39]ca śaknomi: E.
[40]svapuṣpā: A; sapuṣpā: D; sapuṣpa: E; sapuṣpaṃ: C.
[41]milite: E; mīna: A; labhyate: D; taḍate: F.
[42]ca sā: D; ca mām: C; cetasām: A.
[43]tad eva: E, F.
[44]praṇamed: A; praṇāme: B.
[45]vijayaṃ: E.
[46]kṛtvā: C.
[47]vāmorāv: B; vāmabhāge: E.
[48]api saṃsthāpya: B; pi saṃsthāpya: E; tena saṃsthāpya: D; tasya vinyasya: F.
[49]pūjyād: A,F; pūjyā: C; pūjā: D.
[50]yonim akuntalām: A; deyā kulocitā: D.
[51]yonigaṇḍe: A.
[52]tathā manoḥ: B, E; varānane: F.
[53]dadyāt: D.
[54]tatrāṣṭottara-:A; cāṣṭottara-: D; aṣṭottaraṃ śataṃ: F.
[55]tanmadhye ca: D, F.
[56]kucamardana ādau ca: A.

[57]manuṃ mahāstotraṃ: A.
[58]pūjākāle tu kartavyā: E; pūjā tatra prakartavyā: A.
[59]yadi: A, D, F.
[60]tat sādhakottamaḥ: A; sādhakasattamaḥ: E, F.
[61]Śloka 19cd omitted by C.
[62]'Ppi: A.
[63]pūjā prakartavyā: D, F.
[64]Śloka 20ab omitted by C.
[65]Śloka 20cd omitted by C.
[66]tasmāt tv ahetavai yukte: A.
[67]Śloka 21ab omitted by C.
[68]-maṇḍale: A, C. (C^{1}:- maṇḍalam)
[69]After Śloka 21cd A, D insert: puṣpāñjalitrayaṃ datvā praṇamed yonimaṇḍale.
[70]dadyāt: C.
[71]sa guruṃ: B; svayoniṃ: E.
[72]tataḥ: A, B.
[73]-puṭaś ca saḥ: D.
[74]dṛṣṭva: A, C.
[75]jīviṃ: F.
[76]mahāyoner: A, B, E^{1}.
[77]uddhṛtaṃ: B, E, F; uddhṛtya: C; udṛtā: A.
[78]-tantre harapārvatīsaṃvāde prathamaḥ paṭalaḥ: B.

Yonitantra, Paṭala 2

Devy[1] *uvāca* //

(1) devadeva jagannātha[2] sṛṣṭisthityantakāraka[3] /
tvāṃ vinā janakaḥ ko 'pi māṁ vinā jananī parā//
(2) saṃkṣepāt kathitā[4] yonipūjāvidhir[5] anuttamā[5]/
kasyā[6] yoniḥ[7] pūjitavyā yoniś ca kīdṛśī śubhā//

Mahādeva[8] *uvāca*//

(3) naṭī kāpālikā[9] veśyā rajakī nāpitāṅganā/
brāhmaṇī[10] śūdrakanyā ca tathā gopālakanyakā//
(4) mālākārasya[11] kanyā ca nava kanyāḥ prakīrtitāḥ/
athavā sarvajātīyā[12] vidagdhā[13] lolalocanā[14]//
(5) mātṛyonim parityajya sarvayonim[15] ca[15] tāḍayet[15]//
dvādaśābdādhikāyoniṁ[16] yāvat ṣaṣṭiṁ[17] samāpayet[18]//
(6) pratyahaṃ pūjayed yonim pañcatattvair[19] viśeṣataḥ[20]/
yonidarśanamātreṇa tīrthakoṭiphalaṃ labhet//
(7) tilakaṃ yonitattvena vastraṃ ca kularūpakam/
āsanaṃ kularūpaṃ ca pūjanaṃ[21] ca[21] kutobhayam[21]//
(8) prathamaṃ mardanaṃ tasyāḥ[22] kuntalākarṣaṇādikam[23]/
taddhaste[24] ca[25] svaliṅgaṃ[26] ca dadyāt[27] pūjakasattamaḥ[28]//
(9) yonipūjāṃ[29] vidhāyātha[30] liṅgapūjanam[31] uttamam[32]/
candanaṃ kuṅkumaṃ dadyāl liṅgopari varānane//
(10) yonau liṅgam samākṣipya[33] tāḍayed bahuyatnataḥ/
tāḍyamāne[34] punas tasyā[35] jāyate tattvam uttamam//
(11) tattvena pūjayed devīṃ yonirūpām jaganmayīm/
amāvāsyāṃ[36] niśābhāge catuṣpathagato[37] naraḥ//
(12) śmaśāne prāntare gatvā dagdhamīnasamanvitam[38]/
pāyasānnaṃ[39] baliṃ datvā kubera iva pāragaḥ[40]//

(13) citrāyāṃ[41] bhaumavāre ca yo[42] japed[42] yonimaṇḍalam[43]//
paṭhitvā kavacaṃ devi paṭhen nāmasahasrakam//
(14) sa bhavet kālikāputro muktaḥ koṭikulaiḥ saha/
sāmiṣānnaṃ[44] baliṃ datvā śūnyagehe[45] tathā[46] gṛhe//
(15) japitvā ca paṭhitvā ca bhaved[47] yogīśvaro naraḥ/
rajasvalābhagaṃ dṛṣṭvā[48] spṛṣṭvā[49] ca sādhakaḥ svayam//
(16) aṣṭottaraśataṃ japtvā bhaved bhūmi puraṃdaraḥ/
svaśukrair[50] yonipuṣpaiś[51] ca[51] baliṃ datvā japen manum//
(17) dagdhamīnaṃ kukkuṭāṇḍam[52] mūṣikaṃ[53] mahiṣaṃ naram[54]//
madhu māṃsaṃ piṣṭakānnaṃ baliṃ datvā niśāmukhe//
(18) yatra yatra[55] mahāsthāne svayaṃ nṛtyaparāyaṇaḥ[56]/
digaṃbaro muktakeśaḥ sa bhavet saṃpadāṃ[57] padam//
(19) parayonau japen mantram sarvakāle[58] ca[58] sarvadā/
devībuddhyā yajed[59] devīṃ[60] tāṃ śaktiṃ śaktirūpiṇīm//
(20) dharmārthakāmamokṣārthī[61] caturvargaṃ[62] labhen[62] naraḥ[62]/
madyaṃ māṃsaṃ baliṃ dadyān niśāyāṃ sādhakaiḥ saha//
(21) yatnatas tāḍayed yoniṃ kucamardanapūrvakam/
śaktirūpā ca sā devī viparītaratā[63] yadi[64]//
(22) tadā koṭikulaiḥ sākaṃ[65] jīvitam ca sujīvitam/
yonikṣālanatoyena liṅgaprakṣālanena[66] ca//
(23) pūjayitvā mahāyonim[67] arghyam dadyād[68] vidhānataḥ/
tat[69] toyaṃ[69] trividhaṃ[69] kṛtvā bhāgaṃ śaktiyai nivedayet//
(24) bhāgadvayaṃ tathā mantrī[70] kāraṇena vyavasthitam[71]//
miśrayitvā mahādevi pibet[72] sādhakasattamaḥ[73]//
(25) vastrālaṅkāragandhāyais toṣayet[74] parapuruṣīm[75]/
tadyonau pūjayed[76] vidyāṃ niśāśeṣe vidhānataḥ//
(26) bhagaliṅgair[77] bhagakṣālyair[78] bhagaśabdābhidhāyakaiḥ[79]/
bhagaliṅgāmṛtaiḥ[80] kuryān[81] naivedyaṃ sādhakottamaḥ//

iti yonitantre dvitīyaḥ paṭalaḥ//[82]

Yonitantra Paṭala 2: Variant Readings

[1]śrīdevy: B, E.
[2]mahādeva: E.
[3]—kārakaḥ: A, B, C.
[4]kathito: A.
[5]-vidhim anuttamā: C; -vidhipramāṇataḥ: D.
[6]kasya: A, C.
[7]yonau: C, E, F.
[8]śrīmahādeva: B, E.
[9]kāpālikī: F; kāpālinī: D; kapālinī: A.
[10]brāhmāṇī: C; brāhmāṇi: F.
[11]-karasya: A, B, C.
[12]-jātīyāṃ: A.
[13]vidadyāl: A.
[14]-locanām: A.
[15]tāḍayet sarvayoniṣu: D.
[16]dvādaśābdādhikām yoniṃ: A, F; yonir: D.
[17]ṣaṣṭīṃ: B.
[18]samāpyate: E; āprayet: C.
[19]yonitattvair: D, F; upacārais: E.
[20]vidhānataḥ: C; ca pañcabhiḥ: E.
[21]pūjāṃ cāpi kulocitām: D; pūjāṃ cāpi kulodbhavām: F.
[22]tasyāṃ: F.
[23]kuntalam karṣaṇādikam: C; -karṣaṇādibhiḥ: E; cumbanaṃ karṣaṇādikam: F.
[24]tasya haste: E; tasyā haste: B; tadvaktreṇa: A.
[25]Omitted by A, D.
[26]liṅgadānaṃ: D.
[27]kuryāt: D.
[28]sādhakasattamaḥ: D.
[29]-pūjā: D.
[30]vidhātavyā: D.
[31]liṅgaṃ pūjanam: C; -pūjām: A; -pūjā: D.
[32]anuttamām: A; tathottamā: D.
[33]samutkṣipya: D, E.
[34]tāḍyamānau: E.
[35]tasya: B; tasyāṃ: E.
[36]bhaumāvasyāṃ: A, C; bhaumāvāsyāṃ: B, D, E, F.
[37]-pathe gato: C. (C[1]: -pathagato)
[38]-samanvitaḥ: B.
[39]pāyasānna: B, E.
[40]pārakaḥ: E; cāparaḥ: D, F. (F[1]: paragaḥ)
[41]ALL MSS: citāyāṃ.
[42]yojayed: A; yo yajed: D.
[43]-maṇḍale: E.
[44]sāmiṣānna: B, E.
[45]śūnyagoke: D.
[46]'thavā: B, C.
[47]bhave: E.
[48]spṛṣṭvā: C, F; puṣpam: D.
[49]dṛṣṭvā: C, D, F.
[50]saśukre: D.
[51]-puṣpe ca: A, D;- puṣpasya: E.
[52]kukkurāṇḍam: A; kurakuṭākhya: D.
[53]mūṣakaṃ: A, B, D.
[54]naraḥ: D; Omitted by B.
[55]tatra: A, C.
[56]nityaparāyaṇaḥ: A.
[57]sapadāṃ: A.
[58]-kāleṣu: A.
[59]jayed: E.

[60]yonim: D.
[61]-mokṣānām: B, E.
[62]caturvargaphalaṃ labhet: D, F.
[63]viparītā ca sā: B.
[64]yadā: A, B.
[65]śākaṃ: E; saṅgaṃ: B; sāṅkaṃ: D.
[66]liṅgasya kṣālanena: D.
[67]mahādevīṃ: C.
[68]datvā: E.
[69]tattvaṃ ca trisamaṃ: D.
[70]mantraḥ: E.
[71]-sthitaḥ: B.
[72]taṃ pibet: E.
[73]sādhakottamaḥ: E.
[74]sādhayet: E.
[75]parameśvarīm: D; paradevatām: F; parayovanām: B; parayauvanām: E.
[76]prajaped: D.
[77]-liṅga: B.
[78]-kṣālair: D, E, F; samākṣālair: B.
[79]bhagaliṅgābhidhānakaiḥ: B, E;- śabdābhicārakaiḥ: A.
[80]-liṅgāmṛtaṃ: D.
[81]kṛtvā: E.
[82]-tantré harapārvatīsaṃvāde dvitīyaḥ paṭalaḥ: B.

N.B: MS A has a different order of the Ślokas: 1ab-12ab; 12c, 14d; 15ab-20ab; 20c, 12d; 13ab-14ab; 14c, 20d; 21ab-26cd.

Yonitantra, Paṭala 3

(1) [1]athā vakṣye maheśāni sāvadhānāvadhāraya/
gopanīyaṃ[2] prayatnena na prakāśyaṃ kadācana//
(2) prakāśāt siddhihāniḥ syāt prakāśād vadhabandhanam[3]/
prakāśān mantranāśaḥ[4] syāt prakāśāc chivahā bhavet//
(3) yonitattvasamudbhūtaṃ[5] tantraṃ[6] tantrapradhānakam[6]/
sugopyaṃ yadi tantraṃ hi[7] tvatsnehāt prakāśitaṃ//
(4) pāpāśā[8] maithune yasya[9] ghṛṇā[10] syād raktaretasoḥ[11]/
pāne bhrāntir bhaved yasya bhedabuddhiś ca sādhane[12]//
(5) śaktimantraṃ[13] puraskṛtya[14] sa[15] durātmā[15] kathaṃ bhavet[16]/
pūjayitvā mahāyoniṃ[17] chāgameṣādibhir[18] naraiḥ[19]//
(6) rurubhir nakulair[20] uṣṭrair[21] gajair[22] gobhiḥ[22] śivākhubhiḥ/
siṃhair aśvaiḥ kacchapaiś[23] ca pūjayed bhaktibhāvataḥ[24]//
(7) yonidarśanamātreṇa[25] kulakoṭiṃ[26] samuddharet/
candrasūryoparāge ca yadi yoniṃ prapūjayet//
(8) tarpaṇaṃ yonitattvena na punar jāyate bhuvi/
kramaśo lokam āsādya devīloke[27] mahīyate//
(9) tatra tiṣṭhet[28] sādhakendraḥ śaktyāyukto[29] maheśvaraḥ[30]/
mahāśaṅkhena[31] kalyāni sarvaṃ kāryaṃ japādikam//
(10) pañcatattvaṃ vinā devi[32] yat kiṃ cit kriyate[33] naraiḥ[34]/[35]
tat sarvaṃ niṣphalaṃ tasya[36] ante ca narakaṃ[37] vrajet[38]//[39]
(11) antyayonivibhedas[40] tu[41] yat[42] kim[42] cit[42] sādhakottamaiḥ[43]/[44]
kumbhīpāke[45] ca[45] pacyante yāvadābhūtasaṃplavam[46]//
(12) yonimukhe mukham datvā[47] prajaped ayutaṃ yadi/[48]
ayutajanmārjitaṃ[49] pāpaṃ[50] tatkṣaṇād eva naśyati[51]//

(13) retoyuktena[52] puṣpena[53] svapuṣpaṃiśritena[54] vā[55]/
kāraṇenābhimantryātha[56] dadyād yonau prayatnataḥ//
(14) sa bhavet kālikāputra iti khyātim upāgataḥ/[57]
yonimūle[58] vased devī[59] yonyāṃ ca naganandinī[60]//
(15) kālī[61] tārā yonicakre kuntale chinnamastakā/
bagalāmukhī[62] ca mātaṅgī[63] vased yonisamīpataḥ//
(16) yonigarte mahālakṣmīḥ[64] ṣoḍaśī bhuvaneśvarī/
yonipūjanamātreṇa[65] śaktipūjā bhaved dhruvam//
(17) pakṣyādibalijātīnāṃ[66] rudhiraiś ca prapūjayet /
yoni yonīti yo vakti Pjapakāle ca sādhakaḥ //
(18) tasya yoniḥ prasannā syād bhuktimuktipradāyinī /
yogi[67] cen[67] naiva[67] bhogī[67] syād bhogī[68] ca na tu[69]
yogavān[70] //
(19) yogabhogātmakaṃ[71] kaulaṃ yadi yoniprapūjakaḥ[72] /
yonipūjāṃ vinā durge sarvapūjā vṛthā bhavet //
(20) yonimadhye[73] pradhānā[74] ca[74] cāṇḍālī[75] gaṇanāyikā[76]/[77]
tasyāḥ[78] pūjanamātreṇa[79] mama tulyo na saṃśayaḥ //[80]
(21) kiṃ dhyānaiḥ[81] kiṃ japair[83] dānaiḥ kiṃ japaiḥ[83] kiṃ[83]
kulāmṛtaiḥ /[84]
yonipūjāṃ vinā durge sarvaṃ ca niṣphalaṃ bhavet //[85]
(22) yasmai kasmai na dātavyaṃ[86] mama sarvasādhanam /[87]
svayaṃ yady asamarthaḥ[88] syād yonipūjanatatparaḥ //[89]
(23) sādhakaṃ[90] vṛṇuyād[91] durge[92] vastrālaṅkāraṇādibhiḥ /[93]
pūjayitvā mahāyoniṃ[94] paścād āgatya maṇḍalam[95] //
(24) daṇḍavat praṇipatyātha[96] yonimudrāṃ nirīkṣayet /
yasya yonau sādā bhaktiḥ sādhake[97] ca[97] tathā priye //
(25) tasyā durgā prasannā syāt kim anyair bahubhāṣitaiḥ /
kṣatayoniḥ[98] pūjitavyā[99] akṣatāṃ[100] naiva pūjayet //
(26) akṣatāpūjanād[101] devi siddhihāniḥ pade[102] pade[102] //

iti yonitantre[103] tṛtīyaḥ paṭalaḥ //[104]

Yonitantra, Paṭala 3: Variant Readings

[1]śrīśiva uvāca: D; śrīdevy uvāca: E.
[2]gopayec ca: F.
[3]maraṇam dhruvam: B; mṛtyur eva ca: E.
[4]mantrahāniḥ: B, E.
[5]yonitattvaṃ sam-: C, E, F; yonitantraṃ saṃ-: D.

[6]tantre tantre pra-: E; mantratantrapra-: A.
[7]ca: E.
[8]pāpāt sā: A; pāpaṃ syān: B, E.
[9]yaṃ ca: B; syād: F.
[10]śaṅkā: A.
[11]raktacetasā: D.
[12]sādhake :D.
[13]śāktamantraṃ: C.
[14]upāsyaiva: D.
[15]caṇḍīmantraṃ: E.
[16]japet: E; yajet: D.
[17]mahāmāyāṃ: E.
[18]chāgādimahiṣair: A.
[19]naraḥ: F.
[20]hariṇair: A, F; haribhiś: D; na (. .) nair: C.
[21]cāpi: D.
[22]gajagobhiḥ: D, F.
[23]kapotaiś: A; gardabhaiś: B; kurkaraiś: E.
[24]-yogataḥ: D.
[25]yoner darśana-: E.
[26]-koṭiḥ: E; -koṭīḥ: B.
[27]devaloke: A.
[28]tiṣṭhati: C, D; tiṣṭhate: A.
[29]śaktyāṃ śakto: E.
[30]maheśvari: D.
[31]mahāśak hena: A; mahāśaktyena: C, E, F.
[32]durge: C, F.
[33]kurute: D, E.
[34]naraḥ: C, D, E.
[35]Śloka 10b omitted by B.
[36]devi: D, F; yānti: E.
[37]narako: C.
[38]bhavet: A.
[39]Śloka 10cd omitted by B.
[40]anta-: D; a (. .) yoni-: F; anyo yoniṃ bibharti: E.
[41]yo: F.
[42]kriyate: D.
[43]sādhakottamaḥ: B, E.
[44]Śloka 11a omitted by B.
[45]kuṃbhā-: E; mantrīpāke ca: D; -pākeṣu: B, E.
[46]yāvadābhūtaṃ saṃplavam: A; yāvadāhūtasaṃplavam: C, D, F; yāvadā (. .) tasaṃplavam: B.
[47]dadyāt: F.
[48]Śloka 12ab omitted by B.
[49]yutaṃ janmā-: A; saptajanmā-: B; yāvad janmā-: E; -janmārjitaiḥ: A, C.
[50]pāpais: A, C.
[51]naśyate: D.
[52]reta-: B, D; -yuktāni: C.
[53]puṣpāni: C.
[54]supuṣpa-: E,F; -miśritāni: C; -miśrito: F.
[55]ca: D; naraḥ: F.
[56]kāraṇenābhisaṃmantrya: A; kāraṇenābhimantryatha: B; kāraṇenābhimantre(. .): D; kāraṇenāpi saṃmantram: F.
[57]After Śloka 14ab A inserts: jīvacakraṃ yadā prāpya nānyacakraṃ na pūjayet/ jīvacakraṃ maheśāni na vāhena visarjayet//
[58]yonimukhe: E.
[59]gaurī: D, E, F.
[60]jaganandinī: A, E.
[61]kāli: A, E.
[62]kālāmukhī: B.
[63]mataṅgī: D.

[64]mahālakṣmī: A.
[65]yoneḥ pūjana-: B.
[66]pakṣādi-: A; -jātīnā: B.
[67]yo bhogī naiva yogī:B, E.
[68]yogī: B.
[69]ca: D, F.
[70]bhogavān: B.
[71]bhogayogātmakaṃ: B; -bhogārthadaṃ: D.
[72]yoniḥ pra-: C; yoniṃ prapūjayet: D, F; -prapūjakam: E.
[73]-madhye ca: D.
[74]pradhānāni: C.
[75]cāṇḍāla: B; cāṇḍāli D; cāṇḍāle: E.
[76]navanāyikā: E.
[77]Śloka 20ab omitted by A.
[78]tasyāṃ: B, E; tat: C, F.
[79]prapūjana-: C, F.
[80]Śloka 20cd omitted by A.
[81]jñānaiḥ: D, F; (. .) naiḥ: B.
[82]japo: B; tapo: E; tapair: F.
[83]tapobhiḥ: D.
[84]Śloka 21ab omitted by A.
[85]Śloka 21cd omitted by A, C.
[86]vaktavyaṃ: A, E.
[87]Śloka 22ab omitted by C.
[88]yadi samarthaḥ: A, F.
[89]Śloka 22cd omitted by C.
[90]sādhanaṃ: A.
[91]vṛṇuyāya: A; pūjayed: F¹.
[92]syād: A; vāpi: D, F; F¹ is illegible.
[93]Śloka 23ab omitted by C.
[94]maheśāni: E.
[95]sundarīm: D.
[96]-patyārthaṃ: A, B; -patyarthaṃ: D; -patyā ca: E.
[97]sādhane ca: B; sādhanena: E; sādhatu ca: A.
[98]kṣatāyoniḥ: F; -yoniṃ: E.
[99]pūji (tvā): E.
[100]akṣatā: A.
[101]akṣatā pūjitā: A.
[102]prajāyate: C.
[103]iti śrīyonitantre: E.
[104]-tantre harapārvatīsaṃvāde tṛtīyaḥ paṭala: B.

(1) [1]mahācīnakramoktena sarvaṃ kāryaṃ japādikam/
iti te kathitā[2] devi yonipūjāvidhir[3] mayā//
(2) sugopyaṃ[4] yadi deveśi tava snehāt prakāśitam[5]/
kocākhyāne[6] ca[6] deśe[6] ca yonigartasamīpataḥ[7]//
(3) gaṅgāyāḥ[8] paścime bhāge mādhavī nāma viśrutā[9]/
gatvā tatra maheśāni yonidarśanamānasaḥ//
(4) ahaṃ cātra[10] niśaṃ devi yonipūjanatatparaḥ/
bhikṣācāraprasaṅgena[11] gacchāmi[12] ca divāniśam //
(5) mādhavīyonisadṛśī[13] nāsti yonir mahītale /[14]
tatkucau kaṭhinau[15] durge yonis tasyāḥ supīnata[16] //[17]
(6) tasyāḥ[18] pūjanamātreṇa[10] śivo 'haṃ śṛṇu pārvati /
rādhāyoniṃ pūjayitvā kṛṣṇaḥ kṛṣṇatvam āgataḥ[20] //
(7) śrīrāmo jānakīnāthaḥ sītāyoniprapūjakaḥ[21] /
rāvaṇaṃ sakulaṃ hatvā punar āgatya sundari[22] //
(8) ayodhyānagarīṃ[23] ramyāṃ vasatiṃ[24] kṛtavān svayam /
samudrasya mahādevo[25] velāyaṃ[26] vaṭamūlataḥ //
(9) bhaginīyonim āśritya baladevena[27] saṃyutaḥ[28] /
lakṣmīsudarśanenāpi[29] tiṣṭhaty ekaḥ[30] kutobhayaḥ[31] //
(10) ahaṃ viṣṇuś ca brahmā ca[32] munayaś cāmalāsayāḥ[33] /
ābrahmastambaparyantaṃ[34] yonau[35] sarvaṃ[35] prajāyate //
(11) yonitattvasya māhātmyaṃ[36] ko veda[37] bhuvanatraye /
madhu māṃsaṃ tathā matsyaṃ mudrā maithunam eva ca //
(12) pañcatattvaṃ vinā devi[38] sarvaṃ[39] ca[39] niṣphalaṃ[40] bhavet /
sarvebhyaś cottamā vedā[41] vedebhyo[42] vaiṣṇavaṃ param //
(13) vaiṣṇavād uttamaṃ śaivaṃ śaivād dakṣiṇam uttamam /
dakṣiṇād uttamaṃ vāmaṃ vāmāt siddhāntam uttamam//

(14) siddhāntād uttamaṃ kaulaṃ tatrāpi[43] yonilampaṭaḥ[44]/[45]
sūryakhadyotayor yadvan[46] merusarṣapayor[47] iva[47] //
(15) kulīnaḥ[48] sarvatantrāṇām[49] adhikārīti[50] gīyate /
yadi bhāgyavaśenāpi kulīnadārśanaṃ[51] bhavet //
(16) bhakṣabhojyaiś[52] ca saṃtoṣya[53] prārthayed bahuyatnena/
āgaccha sādhakaśreṣṭha yonipūjanatatpara[54] //
(17) tava[55] darśanamātreṇa kṛtārtho 'smi na saṃśayaḥ /
paśunā[56] saha saṃlāpaḥ[57] paśusaṃsarga[58] eva ca //[59]
(18) yadi daivān mahādevi[60] yonidarśanatatparaḥ[61]/
tilakaṃ yonitattvena tadā śuddho bhaviṣyati //
(19) kumārībhojanaṃ durge kulīnabhojanaṃ[62] tathā /
pradhānadvayam[63] etasmiṃ[63] granthe[64] 'pi[64] ca[64] suniścitam[64] //
(20) antaḥ śāktā bahiḥ śaivāḥ[65] sabhāyāṃ vaiṣṇavā matāḥ/[66]
nānārūpadharāḥ[67] kaulā vicaranti mahītale // [68]
(21) janmāntarasahāsre[69] ca[69] yasya vaṃśe prajāyate /[70]
kulīnas tat kulaṃ jñeyaṃ[71] pavitraṃ naganandini // [72]
(22) pādaprakṣālanaṃ yatra kulīnaḥ kurute yadi / [73]
tasya dehaś[74] ca gehaṃ[75] ca pavitraṃ[76] ca[77] na[77] saṃśayaḥ //[78]
(23) yonilaṃpaṭaḥ[79] kulīnaś ca yasmin deśe virājate / [80]
sa[81] deśaḥ[81] pūjyate[81] devair[81] brahmaviṣṇuśivādibhiḥ[82]//[83]
(24) kulīnaṃ[84] pratidānaṃ ca anantāyopapadyate/ [85]
paśuhaste[86] pradānaṃ ca sarvam tat[87] niṣphalam bhavet //[88]
(25) kulīnasya ca māhātmyam[89] mayā vaktum na śakyate/[90]
kulīnaṃ cāpi saṃtoṣya muktaḥ[91] koṭikulaiḥ saha // [92]
(26) kevalaṃ kulayogena prasīdāmi na saṃśayaḥ / [93]
caturthāśramiṇāṃ devi[94] avadhūtāśramo mahān //
(27) tatrāhaṃ kulayogena mahādevatvam āgataḥ /
tatrāpi ca mahādevi yonipūjanatatparaḥ //
(28) tava yoniprasādena tripuraṃ nihataṃ[95] purā /
draupadīyonim[96] āśritya pāṇḍavā jayino raṇe //
(29) abhāve kanyakāyoniṃ[97] vadhūyoniṃ[98] tathaiva ca /
bhaginīyonim[99] āśritya[100] śiṣyānāṃ[101] yonim[101] āśrayet[102] //
(30) pratyahaṃ pūjayed yonau[103] anyathā mantram uccaret[104] /

vṛtha[105] pūja[106] na[106] kartavyā[107] yonipūjaṃ vinā priye //
(31) anyathā japamātreṇa viharet kṣitimaṇḍale //

iti yonitantre[108] *caturthaḥ paṭalaḥ* //[109]

Yonitantra, Paṭala 4: Variant Readings

[1]īśvara uvāca/mahācīniḥ pūjitavyā akṣatāṃ: C; śiva uvāca: D; śrīmahādeva uvāca: E.
[2]kathito: A, B; kathitaṃ: C, D, E, F.
[3]-vidhiṃ: C, D, F.
[4]sugopyā: E.
[5]prakāśitā: E.
[6]kaulākhyātapradeśe: A.
[7]-garte samīpataḥ: E.
[8]gaṅgāyām: A.
[9]viśritā: E.
[10]cātrā: B, E; cāhar: A, D, F.
[11]bhikṣyā-: D.
[12]śadhyāmi: A.
[13]-sādṛśī: D; mādhavīsadṛśī yonir: F.
[14]Śloka 5ab omitted by E.
[15]kacinau: D.
[16]kacīnatā: B, D.
[17]Śloka 5cd omitted by E.
[18]tasyāṃ: B; etat: F; tat: C.
[19]prapūjana-: C.
[20]upāgataḥ: A, C.
[21]śivāyoni-: A; -prasādataḥ: C.
[22]sundarī: B, F; sundarīm: A.
[23]āyodhyāṃ nagarīṃ: C; -nagarī: D; -nagare: A.
[24]vasati: C.
[25]mahādeva: A, B; mahādevi: E; mahāviṣṇur: D, F.
[26]bilvasya: E.
[27]baladevas tu: C; baladevo na: E.
[28]saṃyuktaḥ: F; bhairavaḥ: C; saṃśayaḥ: E.
[29]lakṣmīḥ: C, D, B[1]; lakṣmyāṃ: E; lakṣmīh (sakrarśalaṃ) vātha: D.
[30]eko: A, C.
[31]-bhayam: F
[32]ahaṃ brahmā ca viṣṇuś ca: B, E.
[33]cāmarālayaḥ: A; cāmalālayāḥ: D; ca mahāśayāḥ: E.
[34]-stambha-: A, B, D, E, F.
[35]sarvaṃ yonau: A.
[36]mahātmyaṃ: A, B, D.
[37]vaded: A; dattaṃ: C; vattā: D; bheda: E; F is illegible.
[38]durge: B.
[39]tat sarvaṃ: A.
[40]viphalaṃ: D.
[41]devā: E.
[42]devebhyo: D, E.
[43]kaulāt: E.
[44]-laṃpaṭ (aiḥ): F; -luṃpaṭaḥ: A; parataraṃ nahi: E.
[45]After Sloka 14ab E inserts:

kaulād uttamaṃ tatra api yonau suniścitam/

[46]cāpi: B, E; madhye: D.

[47]meruparvatayor iva: E; triṣu lokeṣu vā punaḥ: D.

[48]kulinaḥ: D.

[49]-tattvānāṃ: C; -vidyānāṃ: B, E.

[50]adhikārī ca: D, F.

[51]kulīnaṃ darśanaṃ: A, C.

[52]bhakṣyair bhojyaiś: D, F.

[53]saṃtarpya: F.

[54]-tatparaḥ: B, D, E, F; -tatparā: C; yonisādhanatatparā: A.

[55]tattva: A.

[56]paśūnāṃ: A.

[57]ālāpaḥ A; cālāpaḥ: C; lāpaś ca: D, F.

[58]-saṃsargaṃ: D, F; paśūnāṃ saṅgam: A.

[59]After Śloka 17cd E inserts: tasyāṃ pūjanamātreṇa mama tulyo na saṃśayaḥ/

[60]maheśāni: C.

[61]-darśanam ācaret: D.

[62]kulīnaṃ bhojanaṃ: A.

[63]pradhānadvayam evāsmiṃ: C, F; pradhānadvayam evā (gr) -aṃ: D; pradhānayoṣidānandaṃ: A.

[64]granthe 'pi tat suniścitam: D; granthe 'pi suviniścitam: F; granthe devi suniścitam: B, E; kulīnaṃ nāsti saṃśayaḥ: A.

[65]śivāḥ: B, D.

[66]Śloka 20ab omitted by A.

[67]nānāveśadharāḥ: B.

[68]Śloka 20cd omitted by A.

[69]-sahasre 'pi: F; -sahasreṣu: B, D.

[70]Śloka 21ab omitted by A.

[71]jñeyaḥ: E.

[72]Śloka 21cd omitted by A.

[73]Śloka 22ab omitted by A.

[74]dehaṃ: D; gehaṃ: B.

[75]dehaṃ: B.

[76]pavitro: E.

[77]nātra: B.

[78]Śloka 22cd omitted by A.

[79]yoni (lubdha): E;- lampaṭe: C, D; -lampaṭai: F.

[80]Śloka 23ab omitted by A, B.

[81]tatra deśasya pūjanti: E.

[82]-śivādayaḥ: E.

[83]Śloka 23cd omitted by A, B.

[84]kulīna: E.

[85]Śloka 24ab omitted by A, B, C, D.

[86]-hasta: C.

[87]ca: C, E.

[88]Śloka 24cd omitted by A.

[89]mahātmyaṃ: B.

[90]Śloka 25ab omitted by A.

[91]mukte: C; muktiḥ: E.

[92]Śloka 25cd omitted by A.

[93]Śloka 26ab omitted by A.

[94]madhye: D, F.

[95]hatavān: B, E.

[96]draupadi-:D; dropadī-: A, B, C, E.

[97]-yonir: A, C;-yoniḥ: E.

[98]-yonis: A, C; pūjanīyā: E.

[99]bhaginīm: A.

[100]āsādya: A, C.

[101]śiṣyānīyonim: C, F; śiṣyāniyonipūjanārtham: A;

śisyāyonim: D; śiṣyayonim: B; śa (śvinī) yonim: E.
[102]śrayet: C; samācaret: B, D.
[103]yonim: D, E.
[104]ācaret: E; ādharet: B.
[105]tathā: F.
[106]pūjanā: A, B.
[107]kartavyāḥ: A.
[108]iti śrīyonitantre: E.
[109]-tantre harapārvatīsaṃvāde caturthaḥ paṭalaḥ: B.

Yonitantra, Paṭala 5

(1) [1]mahāvidyām upāsyaiva yadi yoniṃ na pūjayet /
puraścaryāśatenāpi tasya mantro na siddhyati //
(2) puṣpāñjalitrayaṃ dadyād[2] yonigarte maheśvari[3] /
janmāntarasahasrāṇāṃ pūja tasya prajāyate //
(3) gurur eva[4] śivaḥ sākṣāt tatpatnī tatsvarūpiṇī /
tasyāṃ[5] ramaṇamātreṇa[6] kauliko nārakī[7] bhavet //
(4) sarvasādhāraṇāṃ[8] yoniṃ mardayet[9] sādhakottamaḥ /
tilakaṃ yonitattvena yasya bhāle[10] pradṛśyate[10] //
(5) tatra devāsurā[11] yaksā bhuvanāni caturdaśa /
śrāddhe[12] nimantrayed[12] viprān[12] kulīnān yadi sundari[13] // [14]
(6) tac chrāddhaṃ saphalaṃ tasya[15] pitaraḥ svargavāsinaḥ /[16]
nandanti[17] pitaras tasya[18] gāthāṃ gāyanti te mudā[19] //
(7) api naḥ[20] svakule[20] jātaḥ[21] kulajñānī[22] bhaviṣyati / [23]
tasyā[24] yonau sādhakendraḥ pūjanaṃ kurute[25] yadi[26] // [27]
(8) tadyoniś[28] cāmalā[28] devi[29] sādhakaṃ[30] bhāvayet[31] tu[31] sā [31] /
yonitattvaṃ mahādevi sadā gātre pramardayet[32] //
(9) tadgātraṃ saphalaṃ tasya[33] muktaḥ[34] koṭikulaiḥ saha /
svaliṅgaṃ bhagagarte[35] ca praviśec[36] ca[36] svayaṃ[36] yadi//
(10) tatraiva[37] mahatīṃ[38] pūjāṃ[38] liṅgayonisamāgame[39] /
śukrotsāraṇakāle ca japapūjāparāyaṇaḥ [40] //
(11) tacchukraṃ[41] yonitattvaṃ ca miśrayitvā vidhānataḥ /
yonigarte[42] sādhakendraḥ paradadyād bhūtivṛddhaye[43] //
(12) tadā śrī[44] caraṇād[44] devi[45] samutpatati[46] te 'ṅgane /
pūjākāle ca deveśi anyālāpaṃ vivarjayet //
(13) kāmaśāstraprasaṅgena tadyoniṃ[47] lālayed[47] budhaḥ[48] /
mātṛyoniṃ[49] puraskṛtya yadi pūjāṃ samācaret[50] // [51]
(14) pūjayitvā vidhānena maithunaṃ na samācaret / [52]
parityaktvā[53] ca tadyoniṃ kṣatamātraṃ[54] ca tāḍayet // [55]

(15) yadi bhāgyavaśenāpi[56] brāhmaṇīṃ[57] milate[58] priye /[59]
tadyonitattvam ādāya anyayoniṃ prapūjayet // [60]
(16) pañcatattvaṃ vinā devi paśudīkṣā vṛthā[61] bhavet[61] / [62]
śaktiṃ kulaguruṃ durge[63] āśrayed bahuyatnataḥ // [64]
(17) paśudīkṣāṃ samādāya[65] yadi pūjāparāyaṇaḥ / [66]
tasya dīkṣā ca vyākhyā[67] ca abhicārāya[68] kalpate[68] // [69]
(18) tasmāt prayatnena[70] devi[70] kulīnaṃ gurum āśrayet / [71]
kulīnaṃ[72] gurum āśritya yadi pūjāṃ samācaret[73] // [74]
(19) tadā yoniḥ prasannā syāt kṛṣṇaṃ[75] rādhābhagaṃ[75] yatha[75] / [76]
sītābhagaṃ[77] rāmacandraṃ[78] tvadyonir[79] iva[79] māṃ[79] prati[79] // [80]
(20) yonikuntalām ādāya yadi rājagṛhaṃ[81] vrajet /
tasya kāryāṇi sarvāṇi phalavanti[82] na saṃśayaḥ //
(21) tilakaṃ yonipuṣpena[83] svarṇasthaṃ[84] dhārayed yadi /
sa sindūramaye[85] devi[85] durgāloke mahīyate //

Pārvaty[86] *uvāca* //

(22) kayā[87] vidhyā[88] pūjitavyā yonirūpa jaganmayī /
kiṃ kṛtena[89] prasannā syād vada me karuṇānidhe // [90]
(23) svayaṃ vā pūjayed yonim athavā sādhakena ca / [91]
tat sarvaṃ śrotum icchāmi mama[92] kautūhalaṃ mahat[93] // [94]

Mahadeva[95] *uvaca* //

(24) sādhakena pūjitavyā yonirūpā jaganmayī / [96]
tayā[97] liṅgaṃ ca[98] uddhṛtya prayajec[99] chaktirūpiṇīm[100] //
(25) bhagarūpā mahāmāyā[101] liṅgarūpaḥ sadāśivaḥ /
tayoḥ[102] pūjānamātreṇa jīvan mukto na saṃśayaḥ //
(26) puṣpādikaṃ baliṃ caiva pūjāsāmagrīm[103] eva[103] ca /
yadi naiva tadā durge kāraṇena prapūjayet // [104]
(27) prāṇāyāmaṃ[105] yonigarte ṣaḍaṅgaṃ[106] māyayā[106] priye[106] /
yonimūle[107] śataṃ japtvā liṅgayoniṃ[108] pramārjayet[109] //
(28) sarveṣāṃ sādhakānāṃ[110] ca susamaṃ[111] kathitaṃ[112] maya[112] /
etat tantraṃ [113] ca[113] deveśi na prakāśyaṃ kadācana //

(29) na deyaṃ paraśiṣyebhyo 'bhaktebhyo[114] viśeṣataḥ[115] /
yonitantraṃ[116] mahādevi[117] tava snehāt prakāśitam //

iti yonitantre[118] *pañcamaḥ paṭalaḥ* // [119]

Yonitantra, Paṭala 5: Variant Readings

[1]mahādeva uvāca: D; śrīmahādeva uvāca: F.
[2]datvā: B.
[3]sureśvari: A, C, D.
[4]deva: A.
[5]tasyā: A, C.
[6]maraṇa-: B; gamana-: E.
[7]narakī: A.
[8]-dhāraṇaṃ: C, D, F; dhāraṇīṃ: B, E.
[9]tāḍayet: E.
[10](cutre) praśasyate: D.
[11]devāḥ surā: C.
[12]śraddhā he mantrayed vidvān: A.
[13]sundarīm: A.
[14]Śloka 5cd omitted by B.
[15]jñeyaṃ: D.
[16]Śloka 6ab omitted by B.
[17]nṛtyanti: E.
[18]teṣāṃ: D; sarve: E.
[19]purā: A; sadā: B, D.
[20]naḥ sukule: A: nāsmatkule: D.
[21]kaścit: E.
[22]-jñānaṃ: F.
[23]Śloka 7ab omitted by B.
[24]yasyā: C.
[25]kriyate: A, F.
[26]sadā: E; priye: C.
[27]Śloka 7cd omitted by B.
[28]tadyoniś cātmanā: A; tadyoniś cānalād: D. tadyonau gamanaṃ: E; tadyonyādhiṣṭhitāṃ: C.
[29]devīṃ: C.
[30]sādhako: C.
[31]bhāvayet sadā: C; tāḍayet tu sā: E; tārayeta sā: D.
[32]pradīpayet: A.
[33]devi: D.
[34]muktiḥ: C; asya: D; api: A, E, F.
[35]bhagatattve: A.
[36]praviṣṭam ca svayaṃ: D, F; praviṣṭayata svayaṃ: A; svecchayā veśayed: C.
[37]tad eva: C; tadaiva: F.
[38]mahantī pūjā: A; mahatī, pūjāṃ: E.
[39]-yonyoḥ samāgamet: D.
[40]yadi pūjā-: F.
[41]tadvaktraṃ: A.
[42]yonigaṇḍe: A.
[43]bhūta-: A; yadi kālike: D.
[44]nācaraṇād: D; tv ācaraṇād: F.
[45]devī: A.
[46]sampat patati: A.
[47]tadyoniṃ lobhayed: A; tava yonimayi: E.
[48]priye: E.
[49]mahāyoniṃ: A, B, D, E, F.
[50]karoti ca: B; karoti yaḥ: D, F.

[51]Śloka 13cd omitted by E.
[52]Śloka 14ab omitted by E.
[53]-tyaktā: A, D; -tyajya: B.
[54]-mātrāṃ: C.
[55]Śloka 14cd omitted by E.
[56]-vaśād devi: D, F.
[57]brāhmaṇī: A, B, D, F.
[58]milati: A; milite: B; militā: D, F.
[59]Śloka 15ab omitted by E.
[60]Śloka 15cd omitted by E.
[61]bhaved dhruvam: D.
[62]Śloka 16ab omitted by E. After Śloka 16ab C inserts: OM-kāroccāragā (. .) -māt śālagrāmaṃ śilārcanāt/brāhmaṇīgamanāt caiva śūdrāṃ cāṇḍālatāṃ vrajet/
[6] devi: D.
[64]Śloka 16cd omitted by E.
[65]samānāya: A.
[66]Śloka 17ab omitted by E.
[67]vyākṣā: A, B[1]; yāgaś: B.
[68]narakāyopapadyate: D.
[69]Śloka 17cd omitted by E.
[70]sarvaprayatnena: D, F.
[71]Śloka 18ab omitted by E.
[72]kulīna: C.
[73]karoti ca: D, F.
[74]Śloka 18cd omitted by E.
[75]kṛṣṇa rādhā-: A; kṛṣṇe rādhā-: B; kṛṣṇaṃ rādhā yathā tathā: F; kṛṣṇe rādhā yathā priye: D.
[76]Śloka 19ab omitted by E.
[77]sītāyoniṃ: F.
[78]-candre: B.
[79]tadyonir iva māṃ prati: A, C, D, F; tava yonir mayi priye: B.
[80]Śloka 19cd omitted by E.
[81]rājagrahaṃ: D.
[82]phalanti ca: D, E; phalaṃ vetti: A.
[83]yonitattvena: B, E.
[84]-sthāṃ: D, F.
[85]-mayo devi: E; -maye mantrī: B; vittavasya yo sau: D; vittasyāyano mantrī: F; nirbhayam ayaṃ mantrī: A; nirjñasyayamaṃ mantrī: C.
[86]śrīpārvaty: B, D, E.
[87]kena: A, C, D, E, F.
[88]vidhā: A, B, C, E, F; vidhinā: D.
[89]kṛte ca: D, F; jñāte ca: C.
[90]Śloka 22cd omitted by E.
[91]Śloka 23ab omitted by B, E.
[92]paraṃ: A.
[93]mama: A.
[94]Śloka 23cd omitted by B, E.
[95]śrīmahādeva: B, E, F.
[96]Śloka 24ab omitted by B, E.
[97]atha: E.
[98]sam-: B, E.
[99]pūjayec: C, E, F.
[100]bhaktirūpiṇīm: B, E.
[101]mahāyonir: A.
[102]tasya: A; tat: F. (F[1]: tatat)
[103]-samagrim eva: C; -sāmagrim eva: F; sāmagry asya tathaiva: B; sāmagrāṇi tathaiva: E.
[104]After Śloka 26cd B, F insert: manunā (F: mannāmnā) kevalenāpi tadā yoniṃ prapūjayet/

[105]-yāmo: B.
[106]ṣaḍaṅgaṃ na manuṃ priye: B; ṣaḍaṅgaṃ sumanā priye: E; ṣaḍaṅgam ācaret priye: F; ṣaḍaṅganyāsam ācaret: D.
[107]yoniliṅga: D.
[108]-liṅgair: A;-liṅge: B, E.
[109]pramārdayet: E; prapūjayet: D.
[110]sādhanānāṃ: A, E, F.
[111]sugamam: D, F.
[112]parikīrtitaṃ: B.
[113]tattvaṃ ca: A, C, D; tu mantram: F.
[114]nābhaktebhyo: A[1], F.
[115]kadācana: C, D.
[116]-tattvam C;-cakraṃ: E.
[117]mayā devi: A.
[118]iti śrīyonitantre: E.
[119]-tantre harapārvatīsaṃvāde pañcamaḥ paṭalaḥ: B.

Yonitantra, Paṭala 6

(1) [1]snānakāle ca deveśi yadi yoniṃ nirīkṣayet[2] /
saphalaṃ jīvanaṃ[3] tasya sādhakasya suniścitaṃ // [4]
(2) svayoniṃ parayoniṃ[5] vā kanyāyoniṃ[6] viśeṣataḥ [7] /[8]
abhāve kanyakāyoniṃ śiṣyāyoniṃ[9] nirīkṣayet // [10]
(3) etat tantraṃ mahādevi yasya gehe virājate /
nāgnicaurabhayaṃ tasya ante ca mokṣabhāg bhavet [11] //
(4) paśvādiyonimātraṃ tu[12] abhāve ca prapūjayet /
yonipūjanamātreṇa sākṣād viṣṇur[13] na saṃśayaḥ //
(5) svargaloke ca pātāle sampjūyaś[14] ca surāsuraiḥ /
vīrasādhanakarmāṇi duḥkhalabhyāni[15] kevalam[16] //
(6) susamaṃ[17] sādhanaṃ durge tava snehāt prakāśitam /
yonitattvaṃ samādāya[18] saṅgrāmaṃ[19] praviśed [20] yadi //
(7) jitvā[21] sarvān[21] arīn[21] durge[21] vijayī[22] ca na saṃśayaḥ /
kiṃ gaṅgāsnānamātreṇa[23] kiṃ vā[24] tīrthaniṣevanāt[25] //
(8) nāsti yonisamā[26] bhaktir[26] anyat[27] sarvaṃ[27] vṛthā[27] bhavet[27] /
pañcavaktraiś ca deveśi yonimāhātmyam[28] eva ca //
(9) tadā[29] vaktuṃ na śaknomi śṛṇuṣva naganandini[30] /
tava yoniprasādena[31] mahādevatvaṃ āgataḥ //[32]
(10) na vinā kuntalāṃ yoniṃ[33] mardayed[34] yo[34] 'pi[34] sādhakaḥ [34] /
sa mucyate[35] mahāduḥkhād ghorasaṃsārasāgarāt[36] //
(11) bahunā[37] kim[37] ihoktena[37] śṛṇu pārvati sundari[38] /
vaktuṃ devi yonitattvaṃ loke ko[39] 'pi[39] praśasyate[40] //
(12) śivaviṣṇū[41] vinā devi kaḥ[42] kṣamo[42] varṇituṃ[42] bhavet /
kṣamasva mama daurātmyaṃ[43] mātar durge kṣamasva me//

(13) capalena[44] mayā[45] kiṃcid[45] varṇitam[46] tava sannidhau //

Devy[47] uvāca //

(14) devadeva jagannātha sṛṣṭisthityantakāraka[48] /
vīrasādhanakarmāṇi śrutāni[49] tvanmukhāt[50] prabho //
(15) susamaṃ[51] sādhanaṃ deva śrutaṃ bahuvidhaṃ mayā /
yat[52] tvayā[52] kathitaṃ[52] deva[52] nāstikānāṃ[53] kathaṃ bhavet //
(16) viśvāso 'tra mahādevāsaṃśayo[54] 'bhūt sadā[55] mama[55] //

Mahādeva[56] uvāca //

(17) śṛṇu pārvati cārvaṅgi śṛṇuṣva naganandini[57] / [58]
śṛṇu[59] tvaṃ[59] parayā bhaktyā sāvadhānā[60] śṛṇuṣva me //
(18) yasmai kasmai na dātavyaṃ prāṇānte ca[61] na saṃśayaḥ /
svayonir iva deveśi gopanīyaṃ[62] sadā[63] priye //
(19) nigūḍhaṃ[64] te pravakṣyāmi satyaṃ satyaṃ suniścitam[65] /
yasyānuṣṭhānamātreṇa bhavābdhau na nimajjati [66] //
(20) yonirūpā mahāmāyā liṅgarūpaḥ sadāśivaḥ /
retasā tarpaṇaṃ tasyā madyair māṃsaiś ca sundari //
(21) yonyāṃ liṅgaṃ samākṣipya[67] tattvam ādāya sundari /
yonau kimcid vinikṣipya[68] śaktau[69] sarvaṃ samarpayet[70] //
(22) tattvena toṣayed[71] devīṃ bhagarūpāṃ[72] jaganmayīm /
pratyakṣāt[73] tena deveśi brahmahatyāṃ vyapohati[74] //
(23) nālpapuṇyavatāṃ[75] durge[76] viśvāso jāyate dhruvam /
viśvāsāt siddhim āpnoti viśvāsān mokṣam eva[77] ca[77] // [78]
(24) aviśvāsena[79] deveśi narakaṃ[80] bhavati[80]dhruvam[80] / [81]
sarvasādhanamadhye[82] tu[82] yonisādhanam uttamam //
(25) bhuktvā pītvā ca deveśi yadi yoniṃ prapūjayet /
koṭijanmārjitaṃ[83] pāpaṃ[83] tatkṣaṇād eva naśyati[84] //
(26) bhogena[85] labhate mokṣaṃ bhogena[85] labhate sukham /
tasmāt sarvaprayatnena sādhako bhogavān[86] bhavet //
(27) yoninindāṃ ghṛṇāṃ lajjāṃ varjayen matimān sadā / [87]
kulācāraprasaṅgena yadi yoniṃ na[88] pūjayet //[89]

(28) kiṃ tasya sādhanair lakṣaiḥ[90] sarvaṃ tasya vṛthā bhavet / [91]
sūkṣmāṃśunā[92] yonigartaṃ[93] mārjanaṃ kurute[94] yadi //
(29) tasya dehasya[95] gehasya[95] pāpāṃ[96] ca[96] naśyati[97] dhruvām[98] /
kiṃ gaṅgāsnānamātreṇa kiṃ vā tīrthaniṣevanāt //
(30) pūjyate sādhakendreṇa bhagarūpā sadā[99] priye[99] /
bahunā kim ihoktena śṛṇuṣva prāṇavallabhe[100] // [101]
(31) pūjanaṃ sādhakānāṃ ca sarvasādhāraṇaṃ priye / [102]
pañcatattvaṃ vinā devi caturthaṃ ca[103] vṛthā bhavet //
(32) pañcamāt[104] tu[104] paraṃ nāsti śāktānāṃ[105] sukha-mokṣayoḥ /
vinā śaktyā ca[106] yat pānaṃ tat sarvaṃ[107] niṣphalam[108] bhavet //
(33) śaktyucchiṣṭam pibed dravyaṃ vīrocchiṣṭaṃ[109] ca[109] carvaṇam /
evaṃ kṛtvā mahāyoniṃ pūjayitvā divāniśam //
(34) bkuktvā pītvā maheśāni viharet kṣitimaṇḍale /
vidhṛtya[110] ca tulasīmālāṃ[111] kuryāc[112] ca harimandiram //
(35) kathopakathanaṃ[113] kṛtvā[113] śrīharer[114] guṇakīrta-naṃ[115] /
harināmnā[116] jātabhāvo[117] viharet paśusannidhau //
(36) guptā guptatarā[118] pūjā prakaṭād[119] dhanir[120] eva ca /
varaṃ[121] pūjā na kartavyā paśor agre ca pārvati // [122]
(37) puṣpāñjalitrayenāpi yadi yoniṃ prapūjayet / [123]
tasyālabhyāni[124] karmāṇi naśyanti[125] bhuvanatraye //

iti yonitantre[126] ṣaṣṭhaḥ paṭalaḥ // [127]

Yonitantra, Paṭala 6: Variant Readings

[1]śrīmaheśvara uvāca: C; śrīmahādeva uvāca; F; śrī-śiva uvāca: D.
[2]viśeṣataḥ: A.
[3]jīvitaṃ: E.
[4]Śloka 1cd omitted by A.
[5]parāyoniṃ: D.
[6]vadhūyoniṃ: C.
[7]tathaiva ca: B, E.
[8]Śloka 2ab omitted by A.

[9]śiṣya-: B.
[10]Śloka 2cd omitted by E.
[11](. .) yāt: E.
[12]ca: D, F.
[13]siddhir: A, B.
[14]saṃpūjyaṃ: A, D, E; saṃpūjya: B, C; pūjyate: F.
[15]duḥkhasādhyānā: F; sukhasādhyāni: E; sukhamokṣani: B.
[16]ketanam: B.
[17]sugamaṃ: D, E, F.
[18]samāśrāya: A; samāghrāya: D; samā (. .) ya: C.
[19]saṅgrāme: A, C, F.
[20]pariviśed: A.
[21]jitvā sarvān ripūn durge: A; jitvā ca sakalān vīrān: E.
[22]vijayaṃ: D, F.
[23]-mātram tu: A, C, F; vā sareṇa mātreṇa: D.
[24]ca: B, C; omitted by A.
[25]-niṣevanam: C, F; tīrthāni sevanaiḥ: D; tīrthāni sevayed: E; tīrthāni ca sevanam: A.
[26]-samaṃ devi: D; yonau maheśāni: A, F; yoni maheśāni: C.
[27]bhaktiḥ sarvaṃ vṛthā bhavet: C; bhaktiṃ sarvaṃ vṛthā bhavet: F; bhaktiḥ pūrvā vṛthā bhavet: A; bhaktitaḥ pūjayed dhruvam: D.
[28]yonim ātmā ca: A.
[29]sadā: D.
[30]naganandinī: A.
[31]yoneḥ pra-: B.
[32]Śloka 9cd omitted by C.
[33]devīṃ: D.
[34]mardayed devi sādhakaḥ: E; mardayet sādhakottamaḥ: A; mardayed yo hi sādhakaḥ: B; tattvaṃ vāpi ca sādhakaḥ: D.
[35]mucyati: F; mukto hi: E; yukto hi: B; sevyate: A.
[36]-sāgare: A; -bandhanāt; D, F.
[37]bahunātra kim uktena: B.
[38]sundarī: A.
[39]ko 'tra: D; ke 'pi: C; kyo 'pi: A; F is illegible.
[40]prapadyate: E.
[41]-viṣṇu: A, B, C, D.
[42]kaḥ samo varṇituṃ: A; kasyacid vāñchitaṃ: D.
[43]daurbhāgyaṃ: E; B is illegible.
[44]capalāt tu: A; cāpalāt tu: C; capale 'smin: D.
[45]anucitaṃ: D.
[46]varṇituṃ: C; dorā (. .): D.
[47]śrīdevy: B, E.
[48]-kārakaḥ: A, B, C; -kāraṇa: F.
[49]kṛtāni: E; tvanmukhād: A.
[50]tanmukhāt: C, D, E, F; viśrutaṃ: A.
[51]sugamaṃ: D, F.
[52]kathitaṃ tava deveśa: E.
[53]nāstikālaṃ: A, E.
[54]All MSS: mahādeva saṃśayo.
[55]sadaiva hi: A.
[56]śrīmahādeva: E, F; śiva: D; śrīśiva: B.
[57]prāṇavallabhe: D.

[58]Śloka 17ab omitted by B, E.
[59]śṛṇuṣva: D.
[60]sāvadhāne: C; sāvadhānaṃ: A, D.
[61]'pi: B.
[62]gopanīyā: B, E.
[63]tathā: D.
[64]nigūḍhān: B.
[65]na saṃśayaḥ: D, F.
[66]nimajjate: C.
[67]samutkṣipya: B; samādayet: C.
[68]samākṣipya: D, F.
[69]bhaktau: A.
[70]vinikṣipet: B.
[71]viśayed: A.
[72]yonirūpāṃ: E.
[73]praty (uddhā): B; pratyā (. .): C; pratyā (. .)ā: D; pratimudā: E; pratyā (tm)ā: F.
[74]vyapohatu: A, D, F; vyāpohati: C.
[75]-puṇyaratāṃ:B; -puṇyatarāṃ: C, D; nānāpuraścaratāṃ: E.
[76]devi: E.
[77]āpnuyāt: A.
[78]Śloka 23cd omitted by E.
[79]aviśvāse ca: A, B.
[80]narakaṃ jāyate dhruvam: B; rauravaṃ narakaṃ vrajet: D.
[81]Śloka 24ab omitted by E.
[82]-madhyeṣu: C; -mātreṇa: E.
[83]-janmārjitaiḥ pāpais: F.
[84]naśyate: A, F.
[85]bhoge ca: D.
[86]bhagavān: E.
[87]Śloka 27ab omitted by D.
[88]pra-: F.
[89]Śloka 27cd omitted by D.
[90]mokṣaiḥ: A.
[91]Śloka 28ab omitted by D.
[92]sūkṣmā tu: B; sūkṣmā tu nyā: E; sūkṣma (. .): D.
[93]-garte: B, E.
[94]kriyate: A, C, F.
[95]gehasya dehasya: A, B, F.
[96]pāpāni: A, D, F; pāpaṃ vi -: C.
[97]nāśam: D.
[98]āpnuyuḥ: D; kṣaṇāt: A.
[99]sadānaghe: A.
[100]naganandini: D.
[101]Śloka 30cd omitted by E.
[102]Śloka 31ab omitted by E.
[103]hi: B.
[104]pañcatattvaṃ: E.
[105]śaktānāṃ: C.
[106]tu: D.
[107]pānaṃ : A.
[108]viphalaṃ: C.
[109]vīro (. .): F; vīreṇa saha: B, D.
[110]vidhate: F.
[111]-mālyām: C.
[112]kṛtvā: D.
[113]kathakaḥ kathanaṃ kṛtvā: E; -kathanāgaraṃ: D;-kathanaṃ vāpi: B, E; -kathanaṃ (vaci): F.
[114]śrīhari: A.
[115]nāmakīrtanam: A; guṇakīrtanāt: D.
[116]harināma: D; harimūrti: A.
[117]yater bhāvo: F; (. .) tibhāvo: D.

[118]guptāntarā: E.
[119]prakāśād: B.
[120](. .) āra: E.
[121]ravaṃ: D.
[122]Śloka 36cd omitted by B.
[123]Śloka 37ab omitted by E.
[124]tasyāśubhāni: D, F; tasmāl labhyāni: A.
[125]naśanti: A, C; naśantu: B; na santi: E.
[126]iti śrīyonitantre: E.
[127]-tantre harapārvatīsaṃvāde ṣaṣṭhaḥ paṭalaḥ: B.

Mahādeva[1] *uvāca* //

(1) atha vakṣye maheśāni vīrasādhanam uttamam /
yeṣāṃ[2] vijñānamātreṇa jīvān muktaś ca[3] sādhakaḥ //
(2) divyas[4] tu devavat prāyo[5] vīraś coddhatamānasaḥ[6] /
yad deśe vidyate vīraḥ sa deśaḥ pūjyate suraiḥ //
(3) vīradarśanamātreṇa tīrthakoṭiphalaṃ labhet /
vīrahaste jalaṃ datvā muktaḥ koṭikulaiḥ saha //
(4) vīraṃ[7] saṃtoṣya[7] deveśi[8] kim alabhyaṃ jagattraye /
vīrāṇāṃ japakālas tu sarvakālaḥ[9] praśasyate //
(5) bilvamūle śmaśāne vā prāntare[10] vā[10] gṛhe[11] 'thavā[11] /
ekaliṅge mahāyonau jāpyate sādhakottamaiḥ[12] //
(6) sarveṣām annam[13] āśritya kuryāt svodarapūraṇam[14] /
madhu māṃsaṃ vinā devi kṣaṇād ūrdhvaṃ na jīvati //
(7) tasmād[15] bhuktvā[15] ca pītvā ca viharet[16] kṣitimaṇḍa-
le[16] /
sarveṣām annam[17] āsādya[18] bhojanaṃ[19] cākutobha-
yam[20] //
(8) maithunaṃ ca maheśāni[21] sarvayonau praśasyate /
kadācic candanenāpi kadācit suryayāpi vā[22]//[23]
(9) lepanaṃ ca sadā kuryāt paṅkena[24] rajasāpi[25] vā[25] /
sadānandamayo[26] durge vīraś[27] cāpi[27] virājate //
(10) tatsādhanam[28] ahaṃ[28] vakṣye[28] sarvasarvārthasādha-
nam[29] /
snānādimānasaṃ[30] śaucaṃ[31] mānasaḥ[32] pravaro japaḥ //
(11) pūjanaṃ mānasaṃ divyaṃ mānasam tarpaṇādikam /
sarva eva śubhaḥ kālo nāśubho vidyate kvacit //
(12) na viśeṣo divārātrāu na sandhyāyām mahāniśi[33] /
vastrāsanasthānagehe[34] dehasparśādikeṣu[35] ca[35] //
(13) śuddhim na[36] cācared[36] atra[36] nirvikalpaṃ manaś caret /

dikkālaniyamo nāsti[37] sthityādiniyamaś ca[38] na[38] //
(14) na jape[69] kālaniyamo nārcādiṣu[40] baliṣv[40] api /
strīdveṣo[41] naiva vartavyo[42] viśeṣāt pūjanaṃ striyāḥ[43] //
(15) striyaṃ gacchan sparśan[44] paśyan[44] yatra[45] kutrāpi[45] sādhakaḥ[46] /
datvā bhakṣyaṃ japen mantraṃ bhakṣyadravyaṃ[47] yathāruci //
(16) svecchāniyamaḥ saṃprokto vīrasādhanakarmaṇi /
striyo devāḥ striyaḥ prāṇāḥ striya eva[48] vibhūṣaṇam[48] //
(17) strīsaṅginā[49] sadā bhāvyam anyatha svastriyam[50] api /
yad[51] uktaṃ[52] tava[53] sarvasvaṃ[54] sarvatantreṣu gopitam //
(18) vīrasiddhividhānaṃ tu tava snehāt prākaśitam /
dravyabhakṣaṇakāle[55] ca[56] ādau śaktyai[57] nivedayet //
(19) athavā prathamaṃ bhāgaṃ nikṣipej[58] jalamadhyataḥ[58] /
śmaśāne prāntare gatvā śaktyāyukto[59] 'pi sādhakaḥ //
(20) bhuktvā dravyaṃ japen mantraṃ japtvā[60] maithunam ācaret[61] /
śukrotsāraṇākāle ca śṛṇu pārvati sundari //
(21) yonitattvaṃ samādāya tilakaṃ kurute[62] yadi /
śatajanmārjitam[63] pāpaṃ[64] tatkṣaṇād eva naśyati //
(22) pretabhūmer[65] abhāve ca śūnyālayagato 'pi ca[66] /
tadabhāve[67] japen mantrī[68] nicchidragṛhamadhyataḥ[69] //
(23) prāṇānte[70] ca[71] maheśāni na vadet paśusannidhau /
vīranindā vṛthā pānaṃ vṛthā maithunam eva ca //[72]
(24) pañcatattvaṃ vinā durge[73] na vīro jāyate bhuvi /
tasmād bhuktva ca pītvā ca japen mantrī[74] mahāmanum //[75]
(25) asti guhyatamaṃ devi vīrāṇāṃ sādhanam priye /[76]
kiṃ divyasādhanair[77] lakṣaiḥ[78] kiṃ vīrasādhanais[79] tathā //
(26) kiṃ koṭiśatajapaiś[80] ca[81] puraścaryāśatair api[82] /
kiṃ tīrthasevanair[83] lakṣaiḥ[84] kiṃ dānais tapāsapi ca[85]//[86]
(27) bhagaṃ vinā maheśāni sarvaṃ caiva vṛthā bhavet /
yonipūjanamātreṇa sarvasādhanabhāg bhavet //
(28) tarpaṇād[87] yonitattvena pitaraḥ svargavāsinaḥ /
lālayec[88] ca[89] sadā yoniṃ kuntalākarṣaṇādinā[90]//[91]
(29) kroḍe kṛtvā mahāyoniṃ[92] tāṇḍavaṃ kriyate[93] yadi /[94]

tadā janmārjitaiḥ[95] pāpair muktaḥ koṭikulaiḥ saha //
(30) śiṣyānāṃ[96] kanyakāyoniṃ vadhūyoniṃ viśeṣataḥ[97]/
kevalaṃ gandhapuṣpena pūjayed bhaktibhāvataḥ //
(31) iha loke sukhaṃ bhuktvā devīloke mahīyate /
abhāve[98] gandhapuṣpābhyāṃ[99] kāraṇenāpi pūjayet //
(32) pūjākāle ca[100] deveśi yadi ko[101] 'py[101] atra[101] gacchati[102]/
darśayed vaiṣṇavīṃ pūjām[103] viṣṇunyāsaṃ[104] tathā[104] stavam[104] //

iti yonitantre[105] saptamaḥ paṭalaḥ //[106]

Yonitantra, Paṭala 7: Varaint Readings

[1]śrīmahādeva: A, F; śrīśiva: D; Omitted by B, E.
[2]teṣāṃ: A, E, F.
[3]tu: C, E.
[4]dīvyās: F; dīvyan: E.
[5]proktā: B.
[6]coddhṛta-: C: codbhṛta-: A; ca kṛta-: E.
[7]vīra saṃtoṣa: A; vīrasya darśanād: D.
[8]devi: D; cārvaṅgi: E.
[9]-kāle: F.
[10]prāntare ca: B; śūnyagore: D; guhāyāṃ: E.
[11]grahe 'thavā: A; catuṣpathe: D; prāntareṣu ca: E.
[12] sādhakottamaḥ: A, D.
[13]artham: E.
[14]sodara-: B, C, E; codara-: D, F; -pālanam: D.
[15]tadbhakṣyā: D.
[16]pūjayet parameśvarīm: E.
[17]artham: A.
[18]āśritya: B, E.
[19]bhojyaṃ: D.
[20]ca kutobhayam: B, E; cādate bheyam: D.
[21]mahādevi: E.
[22]ca: A.
[23]Śloka 8c omitted by F; added by F[1].
[24]paṅke ca: A.
[25]rajasāpi ye: E; rajasā priye: B, F.
[26]-mayaṃ: B.
[27]vīrasyāpi: E.
[28]sarvasmāt sādhanād devi: E.
[29]sarvasarvātmasādhanam: D, F; sarvaṃ ca sādhanam: B; sarvasarvajā sādhanam: C; yonyo yaṃ sādhanaṃ smṛtam: E.
[30]snānādir mānasaṃ: C; -mānasaḥ: B, F; -mānasa: D; -mānasaiḥ: A.
[31]śauca: B; śauco: C, F: śaucair: A.

[32]mānasa: C.
[33]divāniśi: A, D; tathā niśi: F.
[34]-snānagehe: A; -snānageha: C, D; -geha: F.
[35]-keṣv api: B, E.
[36]na vicared atra: C; vicārayen nātra: B, E.
[37]nātra: A.
[38]tathā: A, B, F.
[39]japet: B, E, F.
[40]nārcādi vā bali (. .): A; nārcanādibaliṣv: F.
[41]-doṣo: A.
[42]kartavyo: D, E, F.
[43]striyaḥ: A, C.
[44]sparśan yatra: E; sparśaṃ ca: F; abhiṣyanaṃ: D.
[45]yatra tatrāpi: F; atra tatrāpi: D; kutrāpi: E.
[46]sādhakottamaḥ: E.
[47]bhakṣyaṃ dravyaṃ: D; bhakṣyad bhuvyam: A; bhakṣadravyaṃ: E; bhakṣanaṃ ca: D.
[48]eva hi bhūṣaṇam: A; paramabhūṣaṇam: D.
[49]-saṅgināṃ: B; -saṅgena: F; -saṅgeṣu: A.
[50]-striyāṃ: C, D, E, F.
[51]tad: A, C.
[52]ukte: F.
[53]bhava: F; bhāva: C.
[54]sarvasve: B, C, F; sasvaddhe: D.
[55]tad dravyaṃ bhakṣaṇa-: D.
[56]tu: A.
[57]śaktau: A, B.
[58]jalamadhye tu nikṣipet: D.
[59]śaktiyukto: F.
[60]tato: E.
[61]eva ca: E; ārabhet: A, C.
[62]kriyate: A, C, F.
[63]api janmā-: A, C, F; janmajanmā-: D;-janmārjitaiḥ: F.
[64]pāpais: F.
[65]-bhūmau: E.
[66]vā: A, B.
[67]tadbhāve ca: A; tadābhāve: C; tadbhāvena: D.
[68]mantraṃ: D.
[69]nicchidram gṛha-: A;-gṛham āsritaḥ: D.
[70]prāntare: A, B, E.
[71]'pi: D.
[72]After Śloka 23cd C inserts: vṛthānnaṃ varjayen mantrī vīrasādhanakarmaṇi/ madhu māṃsaṃ tathā matsyaṃ mudrā maithunam eva ca//
[73]devi: F.
[74]mantraṃ: D.
[75]Śloka 24cd omitted by B, E.
[76]Śloka 25ab omitted by B.
[77]divyam sādhanair: B; mantrasādhane: D.
[78]lakṣyaiḥ: A, B, C.
[79]-sādhane: A; -sādhanaṃ: B.
[80]-japyais: A;-jāpaiś: D, C.
[81]tu: A.
[82]tathā: A, C.
[83]tīrthaṃ ca śatair: A.
[84]kakṣyaiḥ: B.
[85]vā: D, E, F.
[86]After Śloka 26c C, D insert: kiṃ vā tantrāni sevanaiḥ (D: tattvasevanaiḥ) kiṃ

pūjāśatalakṣaiś ca/
[87]tarpaṇaṃ: A, C, D, F.
[88]nālayec: A.
[89]tu: E.
[90]kuntalaṃ karṣaṇādikam: D, F.
[91]Śloka 28d omitted by E.
[92]sayāne ca: A.
[93]kurute: B, D.
[94]Śloka 29a omitted by E.
[95]janmāyutaiḥ: C, D, E.
[96]śiṣyāni: A; śiṣyānī: C; śiṣyā (. .): F.
[97]tathaiva ca: A.
[98]abhāvya: A.
[99]-puṣpābhya: A; -puṣpebhyāṃ: C.
[100]'pi: D.
[101]ko 'tra: C; ko 'pi: D.
[102]bādhati: A; pragacchati: D.
[103]mudrāṃ: A, D, E.
[104]-nyāsaṃ tathaiṣṇavam: A; -nyāsa tadantaram: B; -nyāsaṃ samācaret: D.
[105]iti śrīyonitantre: E.
[106]-tantre harapārvatīsaṃvāde saptamaḥ paṭalaḥ: B.

Yonitantra, Paṭala 8

(1) [1]urvaśyādiś[2] ca[2] yā[2] nārī[2] triṣu[3] lokeṣu[3] vidyate[4] /
vīrasādhanakāle ca[5] tasyā[6] nāthas[7] tu[7] kaulikaḥ[7] //
(2) maithunena vinā muktir neti[8] śāstrasya[9] nirṇayaḥ[10] /
śrutismṛtipurāṇāni vividhāni[11] kṛtāni[11] me[11] //
(3) paśūnām buddhināśāya śṛṇuṣva prāṇavallabhe /
paramānandarūpeṇa bhajed[12] yonim sakuntalām[13] //
(4) viśeṣataḥ kaliyuge yonirūpām jaganmayīm /
yo japet[14] parayā bhaktyā tasya muktiḥ kare sthitā //
(5) sādhakānām[15] sahasrāṇi upāsyānām[16] ca[16] koṭiśaḥ[16] /
teṣām bhāgyavaśenāpi kālīsādhanatatparaḥ //
(6) kālī[17] ca[17] jagatām[18] mātā sarvaśāstraviniścitā[19] /
kālīsmaraṇamātreṇa[20] bhavapāśair[21] na[21] badhyate[21]// [22]
(7) satyam satyam punar satyam satyam eva suniścitam / [23]
japtvā mahāmanum kālyāḥ kālīputro na samśayaḥ //
(8) ya[24] eva[24] tripurā kālī ṣoḍaśī bhuvaneśvarī /
chinnā[25] tārā[25] mahālakṣmīr[26] mātaṅgī[27] kamalātmikā[27]//
(9) sundarī bhairavī vidyā[28] prakārānyāpi[29] vartate[30] /
dakṣiṇā tāriṇī[31] siddhir naiva cīnakramam[32] vinā //
(10) yasmin mantre yad[33] ācāraḥ[33] sa eva[34] paramo[35] mataḥ[35] /
phalahānir aviśvāsāt[36] tasmād bhāvaparo[37] bhavet[37] //
(11) yad[38] atra[38] likhitam devi tantre ca[39] yonisamjñake[40] /
tat sarvam sādhakānām ca kartavyam bhāvam[41] icchatām[41] //
(12) jihvā yonir mano[42] yonir yoniḥ śrotrau[43] ca cakṣuṣī[44] /
sarvatrāpi[45] maheśani yonicakram vibhāvayet // [46]
(13) yonim vinā maheśnāni sarvapūjā vṛtha bhavet / [47]
sarvapūjām parityajya yonipūjam samācaret //[48]
(14) gurum vinā maheśāni madbhakto na[49] ca[49] siddhyati //[50]

iti yonitantre[51] 'ṣṭamaḥ[52] paṭalaḥ //[53]

Yonitantra, Paṭala 8: Variant Readings

[1]mahādeva uvāca: D, F.
[2]-di ca yā nārī: C; -dī ca yā nārī: F; -dyā ca yā nārī: D; -disamā nārī: E; -diṣu jālādhī: A.
[3]viṣṇuloke: E; viṣṇuloke ca: B.
[4]mahīyate: E.
[5]tu: E.
[6]tasya: E; tato: A.
[7]'stu kaulikām caret: A.
[8]niti: E; iti: A, C, D, F.
[9]śāstre: E.
[10]vinirṇayaḥ: E; niścayaḥ: F.
[11]kṛtāni vividhāni ca: D; kṛtāni vividhā mayā: A, F; kṛtāni vividhaṁ mayā: C.
[12]yajed: D.
[13]sukuntalām: A.
[14]yajet: D; bhajet: A, C.
[15]sādhanānām: D[1] E.
[16]upāsakāś ca koṭayaḥ: D; upasthānām ca koṭayaḥ: F. na prasthānām ca koṭayaḥ: A.
[17]kālikā: E; kalikā: A.
[18]bhajatām: A.
[19]-śāstre viniścitā: D;- viniścitam: A.
[20]tasyā smaraṇa-: D; kālikāsmṛtimātreṇa: B, E.
[21]sarvapāpaiḥ pramucyate: B, E; na ca pāśena badhyate: D.
[22]Śloka 6cd omitted by A.
[23]Śloka 7ab omitted by A, B.
[24]ya eva: A, B; yatraiva: E.
[25]mahātārā: F; mahāmātā: D.
[26]māhāmāyā: B.
[27]kamaḷāmbikā mātaṅgī: F.
[28]bālā: D; devyā: E.
[29]prakārā na: D; prakārānyo 'pi: E; prakārānyā: F; prakārāṇy api: B; prakāśāny api: A.
[30]pravartate: D, F; vidyate: C, E.
[31]tariṇī: A, B, D, E, F.
[32]cīracakram: E.
[33]yathācāraḥ: E.
[34]ekaḥ: D.
[35]paramottamaḥ; A, D.
[36]aviśvāsam: A; aviśvāse: C, D; ca viśvāsāt: B, E; tu viśvāsāt: F.
[37]bhavaparo bhavet: C; bhaktiparāyāṇaḥ: D.
[38]yatra yatra: D; yac chāstram: B, E.
[39]'smin: D, F.
[40]-samjñike: D; -saṅgame: F.
[41]bhāvam icchatā: A, C, F; bhāvaniścitam: D.
[42]mukham: D.
[43]śrotre: B, C, E
[44]cakṣuṣi A, E.
[45]sarvatra ca: A.
[46]Śloka 12d omitted by A.
[47]Śloka 13ab omitted by A.
[48]Śloka 13cd omitted by A, D, F.
[49]nāpi: B, E.
[50]Śloka 14a omitted by A; for Śloka 14b D reads: tathā

mantro na sidhyati/; after Śloka 14ab A inserts: upadeśam vinā devi tathā mantro na sidhyati/

[51]iti śrīyonitantre: E.

[52]-tantre aṣṭamaḥ: A, D, E, F.

[3]-tantre harapārvatīsamvāde 'ṣṭamaḥ paṭalaḥ: B; A concludes: sampūrṇam samāptam; E concludes: samāpto 'yam granthaḥ/ OṂ bhavānyai namaḥ/ OṂ gurave namaḥ/ OṂ kālyai namaḥ/ OṂ śivāya namaḥ// F concludes: iti samāptam.

APPENDIX

Śloka's of the Yonitantra common with other texts:

I., 8cd	: *Bṛhadyonitantra* Folio 6A.
II, 3-4ab	: *Rudrayāmalatantra* (vide: Introduction, p. 20).
II, 5ab (MS D!)	: *Yoginītantra* VI, 44ab.
II, 5cd	: *Yoginītantra* VI, 45cd.
III, 17cd; 18ab	: *Bṛhadyonitantra* Folio 3B.
III, 18cd; 19ab	: *Kulārṇavatantra* II, 23.
III, 25cd; 26ab (MS C!)	: *Yoginītantra* VI, 44cd; 45ab.
IV, 2ab	: *Yoginītantra* XIII, 2ab.
IV, 4cd	: *Yoginītantra* XIII, 4ab.
IV, 5cd	: *Yoginītantra* XIII, 3cd.
IV, 12cd-14ab (MS E!)	: *Kulārṇavatantra* II, 7-8.
IV, 14cd	: *Kulārṇavatantra* II, 16ab.
IV, 20	: *Śyāmārahasya* (vide: Introduction, p. 16).
VI, 33ab	: *Kulārṇavatantra* VIII, 23ab.

BIBLIOGRAPHY

AVALON, A., *Tantra of the Great Liberation* (1913; repr. New York, 1972).

———, *Principles of Tantra* (1914; repr. Madras, 1952).

BEAL, S., *Chinese Accounts of India*, 4 vol. (1883; repr. Calcutta, 1957-8).

BHATTACHARYYA, N.N., *Indian Mother Goddess* (Calcutta, 1971).

———, *History of the Śākta Religion* (New Delhi, 1974).

BRIGGS, G.W., *Gorakhnāth and the Kānpaṭa Yogīs* (1938; repr. New Delhi, 1973).

CAPWELL, C.H., 'The Esoteric Belief of the Bauls of Bengal' in *JAS*, 33 No. 2 (1974), pp. 255-64.

DASGUPTA, S.B., *Obscure Religious Cults* (Calcutta, 1946).

DASH, M.P., *A Descriptive Catalogue of Sanskrit Manuscripts of Orissa* (Bhubaneswar, 1965).

DEY, N.L., *The Geographical Dictionary of Ancient and Mediaeval India* (1927; repr. New Delhi, 1971).

DIMOCK, E.C., *The Place of the Hidden Moon* (Chicago, 1966).

GAIT, E., *A History of Assam.* (Calcutta, 1926).

Gīta Govinda (=Lalit Kalā Series Port Folio No. 15; New Delhi, 1967).

GONDA, J., 'Sanskrit Bhaginī—"Soeur"', in: *Acta Orientalia*, 21 (1953), pp. 23-25.

———, *Aspects of Early Viṣṇuism* (1954; repr. New Delhi, 1969).

GOUDRIAAN, T. and HOOYKAAS, C., *Stuti and Stava* (Amsterdam, 1971).

HAZRA, R.C., *Studies in the Upapurāṇas*, vol. II (Calcutta, 1963).

KAKATI, B.K., *The Mother Goddess Kāmākhyā* (Gauhati, 1948).

VAN KOOY, K.R., *Worship of the Goddess According to the Kālikāpurāṇa* (Leiden, 1972).

LORENZEN, D.N., *The Kāpālikas And Kālāmukhas* (New Delhi, 1972).

LOWIS, L., *Familiar Indian Flowers* (London, 1879).

MITRA, R., *Notices of Sanskrit Manuscripts*, First Series vol. X.1. (Calcutta, 1892).

MONIER-WILLIAMS, M., *Hinduism* (1877; repr. Calcutta, 1951).

SCHOTERMAN, J.A., 'Some Remarks on the Kubjikāmatatantra', in: *ZDMG*, Supplement III. 2 (1977), pp. 932-940.

SHASTRI, H., *A Descriptive Catalogue of the Sanskrit Manuscripts in the Collections of the Royal Asiatic Society of Bengal* (rev. and edited by Ch. Chakravarti), vol. VIII, part I (Calcutta, 1939).

SIRCAR, D.C., *The Śākta Pīṭhas* (sec. rev. ed. New Delhi, 1973).

WILSON, H.H., *Works*, vol. I (London, 1862).

SANSKRIT TEXTS

Agnipurāṇa: ed. by Āchārya Baladeva Upādhyāya (Benares, 1966).

Ṛgvedasamhitā: ed by F. Max Müller, 4 vol. (1890; repr. Benares, 1966).

Kālikāpurāṇa: ed by Śrīviśvanārāyaṇa Śāstrī (Benares, 1972).

Kulārṇavatantra: ed by T. Vidyāratna (1916; repr. Madras, 1965).

Gayāmāhātmya: ed. by the Kailāśa Pustakālaya (Gayā, no date).

Gorakṣaśataka: trans. by G.W. Briggs (vide; Briggs, 1973, Ch. XIV).

Caturvargacintāmaṇi: ed. by Paṇḍit Bharatachandra Śiromaṇi (Calcutta, 1878).

Tripurārahasya: ed. by Paṇḍit Śrīmukunda Śāstrī (Benares, 1932).

Nīlatantra: MS No. 183 in the collections of the RASB.

Padmapurāṇa: ed. by Mahādeva Cimaṇājī Apṭe (1893).

Bṛhadāraṇyaka Upaniṣad : ed. by The Gītāpress (Gorakhpur, Samvat 2012).

Bṛhadyonitantra: MS No. 1389 of the Baṅgīya Sāhitya Pariṣad (Calcutta).

Bhāgavatapurāṇa: ed. by Nārāyaṇa Rāma Āchārya "Kāvyatīrtha" (Bombay, 1950).

Manusmṛti: ed. by Nārāyaṇa Rāma Āchārya "Kāvyatīrtha" (Bombay, 1946).

Mahānirvāṇatantra: ed. by Jīvānanda Vidyāsāgara (Calcutta, 1884).

Mātṛkābhedatantra: ed: by Chintamani Bhattacharya (Calcutta, 1933).

Yoginītantra: ed. by Gaṅgāviṣṇu Śrīkṛṣṇadāsa (Bombay, 1962).

Rādhātantra: ed. by Śrīkālīprasanna Vidyāratna (Calcutta, 1928).

Rudrayāmalatantra: ed. by Rāmacaraṇānada Rāma Śarma (Bombay, 1955).

Vājasaneyisaṃhitā: ed. by Paṇḍit Jagadishlal Shastrī (New Delhi, 1971).

Śatapathabrāhmaṇa: ed. by A. Weber (1849; repr. Benares, 1964).

Śivasaṃhitā: (Calcutta, 1917).

Saṭsāhasrasaṃhitā: MS No. 5-428/54 of the National Archives (Kathmandu, Nepal).

Samayācāratantra: MS No. 31 in the collections of the RASB.

Haṭhayogpradīpikā: ed. and trans. by Pancham Singh (1915; repr. New York, 1974).

Hevajratantra: ed. and trans. by D.L. Snellgrove, 2 vol. (London, 1971).